The Cybersecurity Field guide

A Real-World Roadmap to Breaking In, Leveling Up, and
Thriving in Cyber

Christopher Quimbaya

CISSP CISM

For my brothers and sisters in arms,
who continue to serve—on the battlefield and in cyberspace.

Contents

About the Author

Christopher Quimbaya is a cybersecurity consultant, US Army veteran and founder of the start-up CyberTroopers LLC. He has worked in the Information Technology and Cybersecurity field for over 15 years and has spent his career learning and mentoring others, from soldiers to junior analysts.

He holds degrees in cybersecurity and Information technology and holds multiple industry recognized certifications such as the CISSP, CISM, CEH, SSCP, Security+ and others.

This is Christopher first book in his goal to help as many people as possible make the move to cybersecurity. When he's not dealing with cybersecurity, he is a devoted husband and father of two little girls.

Introduction

Would you believe me if I told you my journey into tech started with a game called *Oregon Trail*?
Well, it did.

I was in kindergarten in the early '90s. It was the first time I ever used a computer, and I was in awe of this 2D green screen game. It might seem silly today with the kind of games we have now, but back then, *Oregon Trail* was the latest and greatest.

From there, my interest in all things' tech exploded.

Computers became a hobby that took up a big chunk of my youth—building gaming PCs and making cash by fixing neighbors' and family members' machines. I've always been good at troubleshooting, and that skill came in handy when I joined the U.S. Army.

While in the Army, I worked on everything from PCs, routers, and switches to radios and even satellites. If it had power, there was a good chance I'd troubleshot it at some point.

It was also the first time I was exposed to the concept of cybersecurity. Sure, I had a rough idea of what viruses were, but I didn't realize there was an entire field that covered much more than just malware. Using cryptographic keys on radios, encrypting network traffic, writing standard operating procedures, and documenting incidents—all of that falls under cybersecurity.

That's when I made it my goal to pursue cybersecurity as a career.

It wasn't easy. I didn't have a game plan or a clear roadmap. I made a lot of mistakes, learned through trial and error, and often wished there was a guide that explained how to break into this field the right way.

That brings us to why this book was born.

Why This Book Exist?

When I started my cybersecurity journey, there weren't many books or resources that really broke down how to get into the field. To be honest, there still aren't.

Sure, some YouTubers offer advice—but many haven't had real careers in cybersecurity. Some have never worked a SOC shift or written an actual incident report.

This book is different. It's based on my experience—starting from the bottom and working my way up over the years.

I wrote this field guide to help others break into cybersecurity and thrive in it. I want people to understand that this field isn't just for "techies" or "nerds." There's room for everyone.

Cybersecurity has a massive talent shortage worldwide. If I can help even a few of you find your place in this field, then my job is done.

Who Is This Book For?

This book is for anyone who wants to break into cybersecurity—whether you're just starting out or making a career shift. You don't need a tech degree. You don't need years of experience. What you do need is drive.

There's a huge shortage of cybersecurity professionals, and there's room for people from every background. But there's a catch: this isn't a shortcut or a cheat code. If you're looking for an easy path, this isn't it.

This book is for people who are ready to show up, put in the work, and push through the hard parts. People who understand that progress comes from effort—not excuses.

I live by a simple motto: **No excuses, just results.** It's something I drilled into my soldiers, and it applies here too. Nobody cares why something didn't go your way. What matters is what you do next.

If that mindset speaks to you, then this book is yours.

Let's get to work.

Chapter 1

Why Cybersecurity?

Cybersecurity wasn't always the hot topic it is today. Back in the day, most people thought it was just about fighting viruses or locking down a computer with antivirus software. Fast forward to now, and everything is online—our banks, hospitals, even our cars. That means a growing need for people who can protect all that. Cybersecurity isn't just some cool tech job anymore; it's a mission. There's never been a better time to jump in. Whether you're looking for job security, meaningful work, or just a new challenge, cybersecurity checks every box.

The World has Gone Digital

The old world of working analog with pen, paper, and filing cabinets is dead. Almost every industry and sector has transitioned or is in the process of going digital. Hospitals run on cloud-based patient systems. Banks rely on real-time online transactions. Even farming equipment is now connected to the internet. Technology has rewritten how we live, work, and communicate.

And with that comes risk.

As more organizations adopt remote work, move operations to the cloud, and rely on smart devices (IoT), their attack surfaces grow. Every laptop connected from a coffee shop, every file stored in a shared cloud drive, and every unsecured smart device adds one more opening for a potential attacker. Businesses wanted speed and convenience—and they got it—but often at the cost of security.

When COVID-19 hit in 2020, everything changed almost overnight. Entire companies had to shift to remote work with little to no warning. They scrambled to set up VPNs, cloud-based tools, and remote access systems just to keep things running. Cybersecurity became an afterthought. Something you'll realize in this field is that many companies don't understand the importance of cybersecurity professionals until something serious happens, like a major breach.

When the world reopened, remote work remained. Companies realized they could cut costs, expand their talent pool, and give employees more flexibility. But that also meant a permanent shift in how cybersecurity had to be approached. Instead of securing a single office network, companies now had to protect dozens—or even hundreds—of home offices, personal devices, and external cloud platforms.

The bad guys took full advantage. Phishing scams and ransomware attacks have been around for years, but they exploded with so many people working remotely. The threat landscape shifted, and it hasn't slowed down.

Let's recall a few major breaches you probably heard about on the news:

Equifax, which exposed the personal data of over 140 million

Americans; Colonial Pipeline, which shut down a critical fuel supply on the East Coast; and SolarWinds, which allowed attackers to spy on government agencies and major corporations. Breaches are inevitable. No system is 100% secure—but many of these incidents were preventable.

Simple things like patching systems, monitoring for anomalies, and enforcing multi-factor authentication could've stopped or limited the damage. But too often, cybersecurity is treated like a luxury—something to "get around to later."

That mindset has cost companies and governments billions of dollars in losses and downtime.

Every business—big or small—needs cybersecurity built into its foundation, not bolted on after the fact. Protecting data is just one part of it. Cybersecurity ensures operations keep running, trust is maintained, and real-world consequences are prevented. Whether it's a hospital saving lives, a small business trying to survive, or a government agency protecting infrastructure—security is no longer optional.

The digital world isn't going backward. It's only expanding, and that means the demand for skilled cybersecurity professionals will keep growing.

Cybercrime Is Booming — But So Is Opportunity

If what comes to mind when you hear "cybersecurity" is some kid in a hoodie hacking away in their mom's basement, that mindset is outdated. Today's cyber threats are run by organized crime groups, ransomware gangs, and nation-state actors. These aren't bored teenagers. These are highly organized operations, with payroll departments, R&D teams, and even customer service for victims.

And they're not just in it to cause chaos. They're after money, data, control, and power.

Victim of A Crime

When I was stationed in Italy back in 2015, I became a victim of identity theft. My brother mentioned over the phone that I had received a letter. It was a notice about an unemployment application being denied. That was confusing—I'd been employed since I was 18 and never applied for unemployment.

Then it got worse. Someone opened a Home Depot credit card in my name for $6,000. There wasn't even a Home Depot in Italy. I had to scramble to cancel the card, put fraud alerts on my credit, and sign up for LifeLock. That was nearly a decade ago. Cybercriminals have only gotten smarter, faster, and more sophisticated since.

According to Cybersecurity Ventures, the cost of cybercrime worldwide could exceed $10.5 trillion annually by 2025—more than the global trade of all major illegal drugs combined.

The 2023 Unit 42 Ransomware Report by Palo Alto Networks revealed that the average ransom payment now exceeds $1.5 million per incident. Criminals are locking out hospitals, school districts, and entire city governments—then demanding cryptocurrency like it's just another Tuesday.

The upside? As the threat landscape grows, so does the need for defenders. That same Cybersecurity Ventures report shows over 3.5 million unfilled cybersecurity jobs worldwide. That number is only growing. Organizations of every kind are desperate for people who can protect their systems, people, and data.

This is your time to shine, and you don't need to be a hacker or a coding genius to get started. You need curiosity, commitment, and a willingness to learn.

Cybersecurity needs defenders, analysts, auditors, engineers, communicators, and policy writers. It's one of the rare industries where your background can be your advantage.

Yes, cybercrime is booming—but so is the opportunity to build a career that's high-impact, high-demand, and future-proof.

The Demand Is Real — And It's Not Slowing Down

Millions of open jobs sound like a great opportunity. But let's break down what that really means.

Cybersecurity isn't just growing—it's exploding across every industry. It's not just tech companies hiring. Hospitals, banks, schools, manufacturers, retailers, airports, and governments all need cybersecurity professionals.

Every time a company stores data, processes payments, connects a device to the internet, or hires a remote worker, they're creating risk. That means they need someone to manage it.

That someone could be you.

The U.S. Bureau of Labor Statistics predicts cybersecurity roles will grow over 30% through 2032—much faster than most other sectors. Companies are paying well to find and keep qualified talent.

This demand is global and remote-friendly. With the right skills and work ethic, you can work from home, earn a solid income, and collaborate with teams worldwide.

Cybersecurity isn't just a "safe job"—it's a smart one. It offers growth, flexibility, and purpose.

It's Not Just for Hackers

Cybersecurity is not just for hoodie-wearing, Red Bull-fueled hackers typing in a dark room.

Yes, there are ethical hackers in this field. They do important work. But that's just one part of a much larger picture.

This field includes people who write scripts and reverse-engineer malware, but also those who build policies, analyze risk, manage compliance, or educate users.

Some work in a Security Operations Centers (SOC) responding to alerts. Others build security into cloud infrastructure. Some never touch a command line—and that's perfectly fine.

Cybersecurity needs all kinds of professionals. Whether you're technical or strategic, hands-on or people-focused, there's a role for you.

To get going all you need is to be curious, consistent, and willing to learn. The rest can be taught.

Make a Real Difference

Cybersecurity is very important and not having the right people to apply it correctly can cause horrible things to happen. This isn't just a job where you push buttons and collect a check. You're protecting people, systems, businesses, even whole nations—from real threats. Whenever you block a phishing email, patch a vulnerability, detect suspicious behavior, or lock down a misconfigured system, you prevent someone from getting scammed, hacked, or taken offline. That could be a hospital staying operational during an emergency. It could be a school protecting student data. It could be a small business avoiding a ransomware attack that would've shut its doors for good.

Cybersecurity is the line between stability and chaos in the digital world.

The threats we face aren't just theoretical. They happen every day: identity theft, bank fraud, ransomware hitting city governments, hackers targeting power plants and water systems, and surveillance tools invading people's privacy. These aren't abstract problems—these are real people and real consequences.

And when you work in this field, you're one of the people standing in the gap.

That's what makes this work so meaningful. Whether you're locking down a server, writing a security policy, educating employees, or responding to an incident, you're making the world a little safer, one decision at a time.

If you've ever wanted a career with purpose, this is it.

You don't have to wear a badge or a uniform to protect and serve. You do it with your keyboard, brain, and mindset in cybersecurity.

A Career That Evolves with You

One of the best things about cybersecurity is that it's not just a job you get into, it's a career you grow *with*. This field changes fast, and that means your opportunities are constantly expanding. You'll never be stuck doing the same thing forever... unless you want to be and even then, the job will probably evolve anyway.

One route some people can take for example is going from a Tier 1 SOC analyst reviewing alerts, escalating incidents, and getting your hands dirty. After a while, you might move up to threat hunting, where you're proactively looking for attackers. From there, maybe you shift to cloud security, digital forensics, or even leadership. You might pivot into GRC (Governance, Risk, and Compliance), red teaming, DevSecOps—you name it.

Cybersecurity gives you room to pivot and room to specialize.

And the best part? As you move up, you build both technical and strategic muscle. The more experience you gain, the more valuable your judgment becomes. People will start coming to you not just for answers but for direction.

A cybersecurity career has continuous learning baked in. There are constantly new tools, new threats, new technologies, it never gets boring. That's intimidating to some people, but if you're the type who likes to stay sharp and keep growing, you'll thrive in this community.

Whether you want to go deep into a technical niche, become a thought leader, or build and lead security teams, there's a path for you in this field. And if your interests shift over time? Cybersecurity is flexible enough to change with you.

This isn't just a career, it's an evolving, high-impact profession that grows with your skills and vision.

Who Is Cybersecurity For?

Cybersecurity is for the curious, the problem-solvers, the late bloomers, the career switchers, the "never thought I could" folks and everyone in between. It's for the people who ask *why*, the ones who tinker, troubleshoot, organize, protect, and teach.

It's for people like you.

You don't need to have a computer science degree, come from a tech background, or be young. I've seen people get into cybersecurity after careers in retail, healthcare, education, law enforcement, logistics, you name it. What matters most isn't where you start, it's that you start.

This field thrives on diversity of thought. Different backgrounds = different perspectives = better problem-solving. I can tell you from my own experience a team full of identical minds misses things. But a team made up of people from different paths? That's where innovation happens.

Are you good at communicating? We need you.

Like solving puzzles? You'll feel right at home.

More into documentation and structure? There's a path for you too.

This field needs planners, builders, thinkers, responders, leaders, and learners. You can be technical or non-technical. You can start as an intern or jump in as a GRC analyst. There's space for you here—as long as you're willing to show up, learn, and keep pushing forward.

Cybersecurity isn't a one-size-fits-all kind of career. It's a choose-your-own-adventure story—and the only requirement to begin is the decision to start.

Ready to Take the First Step?

If you've made it this far, something inside you is already leaning toward this path. Maybe you're still unsure. Perhaps you've been thinking about cybersecurity for a while but didn't know where to begin. Or perhaps you've already been grinding, learning, studying and just need confirmation that you're on the right track.

Well, here it is: You are.

This field needs people who give a damn. People who are willing to learn, solve problems, and protect others. It needs people who bring new perspectives, energy, and voices to the table. You don't have to be perfect. You don't have to know it all. You just have to start.

This book is going to walk you through that process. Step by step. No fluff. No gatekeeping. Just real talk from someone who's walked this road—and wants to help you do the same.

In the next chapter, we'll start breaking down the cybersecurity landscape. You'll learn what roles exist, what people actually do in this field, and where you might fit in. But for now, remember this: there is space for you in cybersecurity.
All you have to do is show up and take the first step.

Let's go.

Chapter 2

Understanding the Cybersecurity Landscape

So, you've decided to get into cybersecurity—but what does that actually mean? It's a fair question because cybersecurity isn't just one job. It's a whole ecosystem. There are people defending networks, testing systems for weaknesses, managing compliance, analyzing threats, building secure infrastructure, and training others on how to stay safe. It's easy to think of cybersecurity as one big job title. Still, this field is full of different lanes—and figuring out which fits you is the key to getting started.

This chapter is going to break it all down. We'll look at the major areas within cybersecurity, the kinds of roles available, and what each one actually does. Whether you're technical or non-technical, introverted or people-oriented, there's a place for you here. You just need to see the whole map.

Let's get into it.

What Is Cybersecurity, Really?

Before discussing the job titles, tools, and career paths, let's define cybersecurity *in plain English.*

Cybersecurity is about protecting people, data, and systems from threats. This includes grandma's Facebook account, hospital medical records, or a company's cloud infrastructure, cybersecurity keeps everything safe in the digital world.

At its core, it is a mix of three things:

- **Technology** – the systems and tools we use to detect, prevent, and respond to threats.

- **Processes** – the policies, procedures, and frameworks that guide how we secure stuff.

- **People** – those with the know-how to use the tools and create the processes.

Through these, you will manage risk, expose threats, make sound decisions, and ensure Confidentiality, Integrity, and Availability (CIA Triad) across networks, devices, and data. The *CIA triad talks* about the three pillars of cybersecurity:

- **Confidentiality** – keeps data private and out of the wrong hands.

- **Integrity** – ensures data wasn't tampered with.

- **Availability** – making sure systems and data are accessible when needed.

Everything we do in cybersecurity supports one or more of these principles, which must be applied to everything: banking, healthcare, transportation, energy, education, and entertainment. Every modern business relies on tech; wherever there's tech, there's risk. That's where we come in.

Key Domains in Cybersecurity

When people think of cybersecurity, they usually picture hackers or people watching security alerts in a dark room. That's part of it—but the field is way bigger than that.

Cybersecurity has many moving parts, and each part plays a role in protecting networks, data, and people. These different areas—or domains—are where jobs live. Having a better idea of what these domains are about will help you find your place in the wide world of cybersecurity; here are some major domains:

Governance, Risk, and Compliance (GRC)

The policy and process side of cyber. Its purpose is to ensure companies follow laws, meet standards (like HIPAA, PCI-DSS, or ISO 27001), and manage cyber risk smartly. This might be your lane if you're organized, like documentation, and enjoy structure.

What they do: Write policies, assess risk, handle audits, and report to leadership.

Good fit for: Strong communicators, detail-oriented thinkers, and people from legal, compliance, or business auditing backgrounds.

Security Operations (Blue Team)

This is the defense team. Blue teamers monitor systems for suspicious activity and respond to incidents. They watch the dashboards, triage alerts, and help stop attacks before they cause damage.

What they do: They work in SOCs (Security Operations Centers), monitor alerts, investigate threats, and escalate incidents.

Good fit for: Analytical minds, curious problem-solvers, calm-under-pressure types.

Offensive Security (Red Team / Ethical Hacking)

This is the offensive team that legally "hacks" networks to find vulnerabilities and test safeguards. They simulate attacks to test how secure a system really is. It's hands-on, technical, and highly specialized.

What they do: Penetration testing, vulnerability assessments, red team exercises.

Good fit for: Tinkerers, reverse engineers, folks who like to break stuff to learn how it works.

Incident Response & Digital Forensics

These are the cleanup crews—and the detectives. When something goes wrong, they jump in to contain the damage, analyze what happened, and figure out how to prevent it from happening again.

What they do: Respond to cyberattacks, recover systems, investigate logs, and collect digital evidence.

Good fit for: Folks who work well under pressure and like to solve problems. Also helps if you enjoy writing.

Cloud Security

This domain expands as more companies move to the cloud (AWS, Azure, GCP). Cloud security pros ensure that those environments are configured properly, protected, and compliant.

What they do: Secure cloud resources, implement IAM, monitor workloads, and write cloud policies.

Good fit for: Tech-savvy people with cloud certifications or experience (or a desire to learn it).

Identity and Access Management (IAM)

This area ensures that only authenticated and authorized individuals have access to networks, data, and resources, in other words Access Control. It's not an area that comes to mind often when thinking about cybersecurity but it's one of the most important parts.

What they do: Manage user roles, permissions, and authentication systems like MFA (Multi-factor Authentication) and SSO (Single Sign-on).

Good fit for: People who like structure, processes, and minimizing risk through access control.

Application Security / DevSecOps

As you may have guessed, cybersecurity isn't only for hardware. AppSec pros ensure that code is secure from the ground up. DevSecOps engineers embed security directly into the software pipeline.

What they do: Review code, use security scanners, and integrate tools into CI/CD (Continuous Integration and Continuous Delivery) pipelines.

Good fit for: Developers, coders, or anyone interested in secure software.

Security Awareness & Training

Cybersecurity isn't just a tech problem—it's a people problem since the weakest link in most cybersecurity programs is uninformed people. This domain teaches users how to stay safe online, avoid phishing, and build a security-first mindset across an organization.

What they do: Create training content, run phishing simulations, and build a security culture.

Good fit for: Teachers, communicators, HR professionals, or anyone passionate about helping others "get it" are good fits.

These are just the broad strokes. The deeper you go the more specialized things get—but don't let that overwhelm you. The goal is to show you that cybersecurity is bigger than you think, and there's room for your unique skill set.

Popular Entry-Level Roles in Cybersecurity

There are many routes to get into cybersecurity, and it really doesn't matter if you come from a tech background, pivot from another industry, or just get started from scratch. There are roles designed to help you get your foot in the door and start building experience.

Some of these jobs are highly technical. Others are focused on processes, communication, or helping people. The key is not to wait for the "perfect" first job—but to land a solid starting point that teaches you the fundamentals and gives you room to grow.

Let's walk through some of the most common and accessible entry-level roles in the field—plus what kind of work they involve, who they're a good fit for, and what type of salary you might expect as you begin your journey.

Security Operations Center (SOC) Analyst

If cybersecurity had a front line, the SOC would be it. SOC Analysts monitor systems for suspicious behavior, investigate alerts, and help stop threats before they cause real damage. This is one of the most popular entry-level roles because it gives you a close-up view of how attackers operate—and how defenders respond in real-time.

You'll spend your days digging through logs, analyzing alerts in an SIEM (Security Information and Event Management) tool, and escalating anything serious to more senior analysts. It's fast-paced, often shift-based, and ideal for people who enjoy solving puzzles, spotting patterns, and reacting quickly under pressure.

Average Salary (U.S.): $60,000–$75,000

With experience, this can climb quickly into the $90K+ range.

GRC Analyst (Governance, Risk, and Compliance)

Not everyone in cybersecurity deals with technical tools. Some of the most critical roles happen on the business and policy side—and that's where GRC comes in.

GRC Analysts ensure organizations follow cybersecurity frameworks, regulations, and best practices. You might help write policies, review risk reports, track compliance, or assist during audits. This role is less hands-on technical and more about structure, documentation, and understanding the bigger picture.

This could be your lane if you're organized, process-oriented, and good at writing clearly. It's also a great fit for career changers coming from legal, finance, healthcare, or admin roles.

Average Salary (U.S.): $65,000–$80,000

Senior GRC pros often break six figures.

Vulnerability Analyst

As the name suggests, you will work on vulnerabilities. Scanning networks, devices, and applications, analyze the results, and helping teams apply fixes to issues found. This differs from ethical hacking, as one is passive and the other active. An ethical hacker exploits vulnerabilities.

You'll work with tools like Nessus or Qualys, generate reports, and prioritize which issues are critical and which can wait. This is a solid middle ground between technical and analytical work and a great way to learn how systems fail and how to strengthen them.

Average Salary (U.S.): $68,000–$85,000

IT Support / Help Desk (Security-Focused)

Believe it or not, many cybersecurity professionals started on the help desk. I did. It may not always be listed as a "security" job. Still, it gives you real-world exposure to account management, endpoint security, and user behavior—core pieces of the cyber puzzle.

You'll help users with password resets, Multi-factor Authentication (MFA) issues, and basic troubleshooting. You might also flag suspicious behavior, escalate incidents, and assist with enforcing security policies. It's a great way to build technical foundations and understand how people and systems interact.

Average Salary (U.S.): $45,000–$60,000

Often higher if your role includes security-specific responsibilities.

Junior Penetration Tester

This is the dream role for a lot of newcomers: ethical hacking. Junior pen testers simulate real-world attacks—on networks, web apps, or internal systems—to help organizations find and fix vulnerabilities before the real attackers do.

This highly technical job requires a strong foundation in networking, scripting, and operating systems. But if you've spent time in labs (TryHackMe, Hack The Box, etc.), built a portfolio, and clearly explained what you've done, you may be more ready than you think.

Average Salary (U.S.): $70,000–$90,000

It can climb into six figures quickly with OSCP or similar certs.

Security Awareness Coordinator

People are the weakest link in just about any cybersecurity program. To mitigate this risk this role focuses on educating users, building a security culture, and helping people make better decisions online. You might design phishing simulations, create training videos, or host workshops on best practices.

This path is fantastic for people who enjoy communication, education, or public speaking. It's one of the most underrated entry points into cyber, especially for career changers with teaching, HR, or marketing backgrounds.

Average Salary (U.S.): $60,000–$75,000

Some large organizations pay more for experienced program leads.

No matter which role you start with, remember: your first job isn't your final destination—it's your launchpad. Once you're in the field, pivoting and moving around is much easier.

A Quick Note on Job Titles

Job titles can mean different things to different companies. Here's an example: At company A Security Analyst works in a SOC role, while at company B they work GRC-focused tasks. Always read the job description to ensure you understand what they are looking for and what's expected.

The Cyber Career Path Is Not Linear

If you're hoping for a straight, step-by-step ladder in cybersecurity—something like "Do A, then B, then land your dream job at C"—sorry to be the barer of bad news, but you're setting yourself up for failure.

Most cybersecurity careers do not have a single straight path for you to take; they are more like a road with many exits. You might start in one area and pivot into something completely different. Maybe you take a detour for a few months, circle back, level up, and end up somewhere you never expected.

That's not failure. That's normal in this field.

I've seen people go from the help desk to SOC analyst to cloud security engineer. I've seen others start in GRC and move into red teaming. Some begin as IT generalists and end up doing malware analysis or incident response. A colleague of mine started in customer service—now he runs phishing simulations as part of a security awareness program.

The point is that you are not locked into one path or role. Once you're in, every project, every certification, every team you join, or every person you meet opens up a new door.

If you stay flexible, continuously learn, and keep building real experience, you'll move forward—not always in a straight line, but always toward something better.

Your first role may not be your dream job, but it can be a steppingstone. What matters most is getting in, getting exposure, and staying in motion.

Your career won't look like mine. And it won't look like anyone else's either. That's the beauty of it.

Technical vs. Non-Technical Paths

I sound like a broken record by now, but cybersecurity welcomes people with all types of skill sets. The key is to find where they fit. Some roles will be very technical, while others will not.

To prove that point, let me tell you about a coworker of mine— we'll call him Brad. Before I met Brad, he was installing key card locks at hotels. Not exactly what you'd call coming from a traditional cybersecurity path, right? But he saw an opening for a junior cybersecurity analyst role, studied hard, passed his CompTIA Security+ exam, and landed the job. Fast forward a few years—Brad is now a cybersecurity engineer and holds the CISSP. I've been mentoring him since he joined the company, and I'll shamelessly take a little credit for where he's at now.

Brad's story isn't rare—it's just not told often enough. Cybersecurity roles can look very different depending on what you enjoy and where your strengths lie.

If you enjoy troubleshooting, solving technical puzzles, or understanding how things work, a technical role may fit you best. Roles like SOC analyst, threat hunter, or penetration tester.

If you prefer structure, policy, or teaching, there's a whole world of non-technical roles for you to choose from. Governance, Risk, and Compliance (GRC), awareness training, and policy development are all critical—and often overlooked—parts of the industry.

There are also hybrid roles that sit right in the middle. Risk analysts, incident response coordinators, DevSecOps engineers, they all operate with people, policy, and technology. These roles are perfect for those who can translate between security teams and business leaders, or who enjoy both big-picture thinking and technical details.

So which path is better, technical or non-technical? Neither is better. The best path is the one that fits you. And don't worry about getting stuck in one lane forever. Cybersecurity is one of the few industries where people switch tracks all the time as they grow and evolve.

Cybersecurity in Different Industries

Cybersecurity isn't just for tech giants and three-letter government agencies. Nowadays, nearly every industry—whether it knows it or not—is a digital operation. If a business stores sensitive data, processes payments, relies on connected devices, or simply operates online, it's a potential target. That means more opportunities for people like you to step in and make a difference.

While the cybersecurity core principles remain consistent across the board, each industry has its own issues—its own set of risks, regulations, and operating environments. Understanding those nuances can help you spot the best fit for your background or interests and better prepare you for interviews and real-world work.

Let's examine how cybersecurity plays out across several major industries.

Healthcare

Some hackers see healthcare providers as prime targets, since they hold patient private information, also known as Protected Health Information (PHI). There have been instances of hackers taking down networks in hospitals, which you could imagine puts patients' lives at stake. That's why cybersecurity in healthcare must balance protection with availability, keeping records, networks, and even medical devices secure without interfering with care.

Healthcare cybersecurity focuses on HIPAA compliance, electronic health record (EHR) security, and preventing disruptions to clinical systems. Common roles include GRC analyst, SOC analyst, compliance officer, and risk manager.

Finance and Banking

This industry is often targeted for obvious reasons. You can expect threats like identity theft, insider fraud, and phishing scams. Due to the sensitivity of what this area manages, it is held to strict compliance standards like PCI-DSS and must maintain highly secure networks while balancing user convenience, which is no easy task.

This sector focuses on fraud detection, transactional monitoring, insider threat defense, and regulatory compliance. Expect roles like security analyst, threat intelligence analyst, fraud investigator, or audit and compliance specialist. This could be your lane if you're drawn to fast-paced environments where risk tolerance is low, and precision is everything.

Government and Defense

Government organizations, whether at the federal, state, or local level—are responsible for vital systems like public safety, infrastructure, and sensitive data. This makes them targets for cyber threats from nation-states, hacktivists, and criminals. From election networks to power grids and military systems, the need for strong, reliable security is critical.

If you work in this area, you'll come across standards like NIST or FISMA, handle classified environments, and stay alert to threats like espionage. You might hold a title like cybersecurity specialist, information systems security officer (ISSO), red or blue team operator, or security policy advisor. A security clearance may be required, and roles often come with a strong sense of mission.

Education

Schools and universities—big and small—deal with more sensitive information than most people realize. But with tight budgets and small IT teams, protecting that data can be a real challenge. Unfortunately, that makes them easy targets for things like ransomware, phishing, and data breaches. And with the rise of remote learning, there are even more ways for attackers to get in.

Cybersecurity in education typically focuses on protecting student and staff data (think FERPA compliance), securing learning platforms, and raising awareness. If you work in this space, you might wear many hats: supporting infrastructure, managing incident response, or running training sessions. Common roles include IT support with a security focus, SOC analyst, security awareness coordinator, or security consultant.

Manufacturing and Critical Infrastructure

Industrial environments like factories, power plants, transportation networks, and utility companies depend on specialized systems known as operational technology (OT) or industrial control systems (ICS) to keep things running smoothly. Much of this technology was designed without security in mind, and now it's being linked to the Internet.

Security in these environments should go well beyond data breaches. You're safeguarding physical systems, employee safety, and national supply chains. The threats can be as broad as ransomware crippling a pipeline or as insidious as attackers manipulating a sensor on a factory floor. A few roles to consider if this intrigues you: OT security engineer, ICS/SCADA analyst, incident responder, or vulnerability management specialist.

Retail, E-Commerce, and Media

If a company accepts payments online, stores customer data, or hosts public-facing websites, it's a target for cyber-attacks. They're constantly fighting against card-skimming malware, web app attacks, credential stuffing, and privacy compliance issues like GDPR or CCPA. Data breaches, for them, don't merely cost money—they cost reputation and trust in the brand.

In this space, you'll often find roles like application security analyst, cloud security engineer, compliance specialist, or DevSecOps engineer. Your focus might be on securing APIs, protecting cloud infrastructure, preventing fraud, or ensuring compliance with consumer data protection laws.

Cybersecurity Is Everywhere

You don't have to work for a tech company to have a meaningful and rewarding career in this field. In fact, your experience in other industries—healthcare, education, logistics, retail, or something else—can be a serious advantage. You already understand how those environments work. That insider knowledge can help you secure them more effectively.

Cyber is a bridge between technology and the real world. Every sector needs it, which means there's a place for you, wherever you come from.

Every industry has its own risks, but they all have something in common, they want to protect systems, protect data, and protect people.

How to Choose Your Path

At this point it should be clear how broad the cybersecurity field is. From blue team to red team, cloud to compliance, forensics to user awareness, there's no shortage of directions to explore. But that leads to the question: *How do I know where I fit?*

The honest answer? It's still too early to know if you're new to cyber, focus on learning the basics and about each area before making your choice.

There is no perfect choice, just keep in mind your first job won't be your final destination, at least not for most. The goal is to choose a starting point that matches your natural strengths, keeps you engaged, and gives you room to grow.

A good way to narrow things down is to ask yourself key questions.

Do you enjoy solving puzzles or digging into problems until you figure out what went wrong? That mindset often aligns with threat hunting, SOC work, or digital forensics—roles that require analytical thinking and investigative instincts.

Do you prefer structure, rules, and organizing systems? If you like working with policies or mapping out processes, GRC (Governance, Risk, and Compliance) or risk management might be your zone.

Do you enjoy working with people and translating complex ideas into plain English? You might be a great fit for security awareness, training, or project coordination roles.

Looking for more hands-on and like to get in the weeds of things, penetration testing, vulnerability management, or security engineering may work for you. These technical roles let you build, break, fix, and explore systems on a deeper level.

Cloud security is one of the fastest-growing areas in cyber, and it's looking for people who understand services like AWS, Azure, and Google Cloud—and how to keep them secure.

Don't lock yourself into a single route, you can always pivot into something else. Just choose a starting point that sparks your interest and gives you space to grow.

The Best Path Is the One You Actually Take

Don't spend time making the "perfect" choice. Just do it and tweak it as you move along. Cybersecurity is not a one-size-fits-all profession. It's more like a toolbox — you can choose which tools you want to master.

Whether you're technical, non-technical, creative, strategic, or a mix, there's a role for you in this space.

Start where you are. Use what you have. Learn as you go.

Chapter 3

Skills, Certifications, and Learning Resources

Now that you've seen the different roles and domains in cybersecurity, you're probably wondering: "What do I actually need to learn to get started?" That's exactly what this chapter is about.

This is where we shift from exploring the field to building your toolkit. We'll cover the core skills, certifications, and the learning resources that won't waste your time—or your money. Whether your brand new or already messing around in labs, this chapter will help you focus your energy and avoid the trap of trying to learn everything at once.

The goal here is to build a solid foundation and go from there, no one is expecting you to know everything. Let's break it down.

Core Skills and What You Need to Know

Let's clear this up right now: you do not need to know everything to work in this field. Nobody does. Not the senior engineers, not the CISOs (Chief information Security Officer), not even the folks who write the certifications.

Cybersecurity is massive and constantly evolving. New threats, new tools, new frameworks, it never stops. So, if you're waiting until you "know enough" before applying for that first job or diving into a new role, let me save you some time: you'll be waiting forever.

A few years ago, I took a position as a Cybersecurity Engineer supporting Risk Management Framework (RMF). I felt confident. But right after I started, the lead engineer for the architecture and design team quit. Guess who got tapped to replace him.

Me.

I had almost no hands-on experience in the area of cybersecurity architecture and design. To make matters worse I had no documentation, no processes, no roadmap to work from. Just a lot of uncertainty. I remember sitting at my kitchen table one night, overwhelmed.

My wife saw the look on my face and asked what was wrong. I laid it all out, expecting sympathy. Instead, she hit me with: "So... fix it. What's your motto?"

She was right. No excuses. Just results.

I dove into frameworks, technical guides, and NIST publications. I leaned on trusted colleagues. We built new systems from scratch and turned that team into one of the most productive on the cyber side. I didn't have the answers at first— but I was willing to figure them out.

That's what this field demands: problem solvers. You don't need to be a subject matter expert on day one. What you do need is a strong foundation, a willingness to learn, and the humility to ask for help.

What are the skills needed to form a cybersecurity foundation?

Networking Fundamentals

You can't defend what you don't understand. Learn how data moves through a network—IP addresses, ports, TCP/UDP protocols, DNS, DHCP, NAT. It's important to have a broad understanding of switches, routers, and firewalls. Once you know what "normal" looks like, it becomes easier to spot when something's off.

Operating Systems: Windows and Linux

Get a solid foundation navigating Linux (commands like ls, grep, chmod, sudo) and Windows (PowerShell, Event Viewer, system logs). These skills will come in handy when you're investigating incidents or hardening a system. Making a cheat sheet of common commands is a good idea. I still use mine. There are obviously more operating systems, but Windows and Linux will be the lions share.

Security Fundamentals

As I mentioned before, the CIA Triad are the three pillars of cybersecurity. You also need to understand threats like phishing, malware, brute-force attacks, ransomware. Learn about firewalls, antivirus software, encryption, access control, and key terms like vulnerability, exploit, risk, and how to mitigate risk.

Scripting and Automation

Optional, but can really upgrade your productivity. By learning basic scripting in Python, Bash, or PowerShell you can automate repetitive tasks like log filtering, scanning, or reporting. You don't have to be a programmer, just being able to write and tweak simple scripts can set you apart.

Cloud Security Awareness

Cloud is everywhere now. Understand the basics of AWS, Azure, or Google Cloud. Learn the Shared Responsibility Model, IAM, and common misconfigurations. Even a basic grasp of cloud security will make you far more versatile. There are more cloud vendors, but these are the most common.

Soft Skills That Set You Apart

Technical skills are essential—but soft skills are what help you grow. Can you write clear documentation? Communicate with non-technical people? Stay calm under pressure? Ask the right questions?

Cybersecurity is a team sport. Be the person others can rely on, especially when things get messy. Combine that with technical skills, and you're not just ready to land your first job, you're ready to thrive in it.

Degrees vs Certifications

Do you need a degree, and does it carry more weight than a certification?

The short answer is no—you don't need a degree to get into cybersecurity. I didn't get mine until well into my career. But degrees do have their place on this journey. You can gain a lot from structured learning, and some universities even offer vouchers for certifications after you pass certain classes—Western Governors University, for example. A degree also checks the box for many roles and can be a bargaining chip when it comes to salary. Some mid-level and advanced roles actually require a bachelor's degree (or higher) just to apply. For certain companies, it's non-negotiable.

I once interviewed with a major military contractor for an ISSM position. At that point, I had plenty of experience, plus my Security+ and CEH, and I knew I was ready. I crushed the interview—but they told me to come back after I graduated. I thanked them for their time and jotted down a few notes afterward. Two months later, I earned my cybersecurity degree. About six months after that, I got a call from the same company asking if I wanted to interview again. I said, "Let's do it."

Funny enough, it was the same interview panel. I still had my notes from the first time around—and this time, I got the job. Honestly, was I any different from six months earlier? Not really. The biggest difference was that I now had that piece of paper. And it pushed me to the next level—along with a bump in pay.

So long story short: you don't need a degree to start. But if you want to level up later in your career, I do recommend getting one.

From here on out, we'll focus on certifications.

Smart Certification Strategy

There are many certs to choose from and you would like to know:
"Which certs do I need to get hired?"

My answer, none of them and all of them. The truth is, it depends on your goals, your background, and where you want to go in this field. Certifications can absolutely help you, but let's set the record straight: they are not a golden ticket. They won't just get you a job or make you an expert overnight, if they did, I wouldn't be writing this book. Certifications should be used strategically; they can do three important things:

1. Structure your learning.
2. Build your confidence.
3. Show hiring managers that you're serious about your growth.

The real key is choosing the right certification at the right time. Not just because it's trending, but because it aligns with your path and teaches you something meaningful.

What Makes a Certification Worth Your Time?

Before you commit your time or money, ask yourself a few honest questions:

- Will this help me land my first role or transition into a new one?

- Is it recognized and valued by employers in the area or industry I'm targeting?

- Does it match where I am right now—and help me move toward where I want to be next?

If it doesn't meet at least two out of three, pause and reconsider. Don't waste energy and resources chasing shiny badges that won't serve your goals.

Entry-Level Certifications

These are completely optional, but they can help you build a better baseline to work from, especially if you're coming from a non-technical background. These certs are designed to teach the fundamentals and boost your confidence on the subject without overwhelming you.

CompTIA IT Fundamentals (ITF+) – A gentle starting point for absolute beginners. Think of it as cybersecurity kindergarten: it covers basic concepts like hardware, software, and IT terminology. Good if you've never touched a command line in your life.

Google Cybersecurity Certificate (via Coursera) – Structured, hands-on, and tailored for career changers. It walks you through security fundamentals with labs and real-world examples. Bonus: it's taught in plain English and is budget friendly.

Microsoft SC-900 – If you're curious about cloud, identity, and compliance—especially in Microsoft-heavy environments— this is a smart intro. It's light on technical details but gives you a great foundation in security concepts.

CompTIA A+ (Optional) – Focused more on IT support than security, but helpful if you're starting from help desk or looking to pivot from a general tech role. A+ teaches you how computers work, how to troubleshoot issues, and how systems connect.

Entry-Level Security Certifications

Once you're comfortable with the basics, it's time to step into entry-level security certs that can help you land your first job in cybersecurity.

CompTIA Security+ – The gold standard for beginners. It covers a wide range of topics including networking, cryptography, incident response, access control, and risk management. Recognized almost everywhere and often listed in job postings.

ISC2 Certified in Cybersecurity (CC) – A newer player in the space but growing fast. ISC2 offers the training and exam for free, which makes this an incredibly accessible cert. It's slightly more theory-based than Security+, but still valuable for resumes and interviews.

Cisco CyberOps Associate – A great cert for aspiring SOC analysts or blue teamers. This cert dives deeper into monitoring tools, SIEMs, and real-world detection practices. If you're targeting a role in incident response, this is worth a look.

Role-Specific and Mid-Level Certifications

Once you've got your footing and maybe some hands-on experience, it's time to specialize. These certifications help you deepen your skills in a specific area and signal that you're ready to contribute at a higher level.

Blue Team / SOC Roles

CompTIA CySA+ – This cert picks up where Security+ leaves off. It emphasizes threat detection, behavioral analytics, and incident response. It's ideal for SOC roles or anyone aiming to work in defensive operations.

Splunk Core Certified User – Splunk is one of the most widely used SIEM tools. This cert shows you know how to search logs, use dashboards, and analyze data effectively—skills that are critical in blue teamwork.

Blue Team Level 1 (BTL1) – Created by blue team professionals, this cert is practical, hands-on, and focused on real-world defense tasks. Great for lab learners and career changers who want more than just theory.

Penetration Testing / Offensive Security

eJPT (eLearnSecurity Junior Penetration Tester) – If ethical hacking and red teaming is where you want to be, this is a perfect intro. It's hands-on and beginner-friendly, focusing on the tools and techniques used by real-world pentesters.

CompTIA PenTest+ – Offers broader coverage of penetration testing concepts, from planning and scoping to exploitation and reporting. Less hands-on than eJPT, but more well-rounded for those who want depth.

CEH (Certified Ethical Hacker) – This one's controversial. It's still listed on job postings, especially for government work, but the value is mostly in compliance. If a job requires it, take it. Otherwise, there are better options for skill-building.

GRC & Compliance Roles

ISO 27001 Foundations / Lead Implementer – Great if you're helping businesses meet security standards. It teaches the principles behind ISMS (Information Security Management Systems) and how to apply them.

CISA (Certified Information Systems Auditor) – One of the top certifications for IT auditing and risk. It's more advanced, but great for folks working in enterprise, compliance, or audit-heavy environments.

ISC2 CC – This cert shows up again here because its broad base makes it relevant to both technical and GRC paths. A good steppingstone for newcomers to compliance and risk.

Cloud Security

AWS Certified Cloud Practitioner – A non-technical overview of AWS services, billing, architecture, and security responsibilities. Great for anyone entering cloud security from the ground up.

Microsoft Azure Fundamentals (AZ-900) – Similar to AWS's intro cert but tailored to the Microsoft ecosystem. Useful if you're working in a Microsoft-heavy shop.

Google Cloud Digital Leader – Helps you understand how Google Cloud thinks about security and cloud transformation. It's beginner-friendly and a nice option for those targeting GCP-focused roles.

AWS Certified Security – Specialty – This one's intermediate-to-advanced. It dives deep into IAM, encryption, monitoring, and incident response in cloud environments. A great goal cert once you've got cloud fundamentals down.

Advanced Certifications

If you're aiming for senior technical roles, leadership, or deep specialization, these are the certifications that will help you stand out at the highest levels.

CISSP (Certified Information Systems Security Professional) – Arguably the most recognized cert in cybersecurity. It focuses on architecture, policy, governance, and risk. Required for many senior roles. Note: it requires five years of experience to hold the cert, but you can take the exam early.

CISM (Certified Information Security Manager) – Best for aspiring security managers, risk officers, or policy leads. Think of leadership and strategy over hands-on work.

CCSP (Certified Cloud Security Professional) – Offered by ISC2 and tailored to professionals working in cloud security. It covers design, operations, and risk in cloud systems.

OSCP (Offensive Security Certified Professional) – One of the toughest and most respected offensive security certs. Very hands-on and very technical. If you want to prove you can hack with the best, this is the one to earn.

GIAC Certifications (via SANS Institute) – Pricey, but incredibly well-respected. These include GCIH (Incident Handling), GPEN (Penetration Testing), GSEC (General Security Knowledge), and many more. Great for those who want top-tier recognition.

Quality Over Quantity

Some people start collecting certifications like they are Pokémon cards, but this is a situation where you don't have to catch'em all. Without hands-on experience to backup your certs won't help your career much, it will drain your bank account since many of these certs can get expensive.

The better strategy? Choose one certification that aligns with your target role. Focus on learning the material. Then apply it— in a lab, a volunteer project, a simulation, or even just a personal write-up.

Certs don't prove you can do the job—but applying what you've learned does.

That's the goal. One cert. Real experience. Repeat as needed.

Choosing a job-relevant certification, paired with hands-on experience, will do far more for your career than five random certs you barely remember studying for.

Pick certifications that align with your goals and the type of work you actually want to do. Focus on one at a time, absorb it fully, and look for ways to use what you're learning—whether that's in a lab, a side project, or volunteering. Anyone can study and pass an exam. The goal should be to become someone who can do the work confidently and competently.

That's what moves your career forward—not the number of logos you can slap on your resume.

Getting Hands-On: Labs, Tools, and Projects

You can only get so far by reading, watching videos, or memorizing facts. Cybersecurity is a field built on doing—and that's where hands-on practice comes in.

The good news? You don't need a high-end lab or expensive equipment to get started. Many of the tools professionals use every day are free, and setting up a home lab is easier than you might think.

Let's walk through how to get practical experience using real-world tools, building labs, tackling challenges, and creating your own projects that show what you can do without having to break the bank.

Start With Free Tools

If you think you will have to buy very expensive tools or software to get some hands-on experience, well you're in luck

I'm here to show how, on the cheap. Some of the best tools are open-source and widely used by many people and companies across the industry. Here are some core tools to build your own home cybersecurity lab:

VirtualBox or VMware Player

Virtualization software lets you run multiple virtual machines (VMs) on a single computer. Set up different operating systems—like Kali Linux, Windows 10, and Ubuntu—and practice attacks, defense, and system administration in a safe, isolated environment.

Kali Linux

This is the Swiss army knife for ethical hackers, it's packed with penetration testing tools like Nmap, Metasploit, Hydra, and Wireshark. It's the go-to OS for red teamers and ethical hackers, and it's great for exploring vulnerabilities in a lab setup.

Wireshark

A powerful network traffic analyzer that lets you capture and inspect data packets. It helps you understand how protocols like TCP, DNS, and HTTP function—and how to detect abnormal traffic or signs of compromise.

Burp Suite (Community Edition)

This will allow you to test web applications. It intercepts and modifies traffic between your browser and a target application—perfect for learning how login forms, sessions, and cookies work.

Splunk (Free Version)

An industry-standard SIEM (Security Information and Event Management) tool. It's great for log collection, search, and analysis. The free version lets you build foundational skills that are highly valued in SOC roles.

Security Onion
An all-in-one blue team distro that includes tools like Zeek, Suricata, and Elasticsearch. Use it to detect simulated attacks, investigate logs, and run your own defensive operations.

Each of these tools teaches you something different. Pick one, explore, break it, fix it, and repeat. You don't have to master everything on this list, what's important is to gain experience.

Hands-On Practice Platforms

I know reading about cybersecurity can be boring, but there is a fun side as well. This will be the most entertaining part of your training journey, especially if you're like me and learn best by doing. These platforms are interactive, beginner-friendly, and widely respected in the industry:

TryHackMe
This is one of the best starting points for getting hands-on experience on many different tools and areas. This platform offers guided learning paths, beginner challenges, and a helpful community. The free tier is generous. Premium is affordable and worth the upgrade.

Hack The Box (HTB)
While HTB is known for more advanced hacking challenges, their "Starting Point" track is beginner-friendly and structured. It's a great next step once you've explored TryHackMe.

OverTheWire
This one's a classic, been around since the early 2010's. It uses command-line puzzles to teach Linux fundamentals and security concepts. Entirely free and a great tool for sharpening your CLI skills.

RangeForce (Community Edition)

This is a browser-based lab environment with real-world simulations. You'll tackle phishing, endpoint defense, SIEM analysis, and more.

Video Courses and Massive Open Online Courses (MOOCs)

If structured video learning is more in your lane, there's no shortage of high-quality, affordable (and often free) online courses out there. Whether you're a visual learner or just want a clear path to follow, these platforms offer solid content to help you build skills at your own pace:

Coursera

Home to the Google Cybersecurity Certificate and many university-backed programs. Many courses can be taken for free, and you only pay if you want the certificate.

edX

Another great platform with free content from places like Harvard and MIT. Like Coursera, you can often learn for free and pay later if you want proof of completion.

Udemy

If you time it right, you can grab top-rated courses for under $20. Look for updated, well-reviewed content on topics like Security+, ethical hacking, cloud, and SOC analyst skills.

Cybrary

This platform has been around for a while and offers free and premium training for security fundamentals, cloud, SOC, and more. Their career paths are especially helpful.

Books and Written Guides

I know far too many people who rather opt for modules or videos over reading a book, I get it. Reading about Cybersecurity is rough I would know I have a library full of them, but if you're this far into this book might as well add some more while you're at it.

I still believe books are still one of the best ways to build deep knowledge. Start with titles that offer practical, real-world guidance:

- *Cybersecurity Career Master Plan* by Dr. Gerald Auger

- *The Pentester Blueprint* by Phillip Wylie and Kim Crawley

- *Blue Team Field Manual* by Alan J. White and Ben Clark

- *The Art of Exploitation* by Jon Erickson (more advanced)

If you have access to a public or university library, check if they provide digital access to O'Reilly or Safari Books. Tons of tech books live there—and they're free with a login.

Show What You Know

You've been learning, practicing, and building—now it's time to let people see it.

One of the biggest mistakes I see beginners make is keeping all their work hidden. You finish a project, beat a lab, solve a CTF challenge... and then quietly move on to the next thing. Don't do that. If you're putting in the effort, let it speak for you.

Your portfolio is proof. It's how you show potential employers that you're not just learning—you're applying. That you're not waiting for permission—you're building momentum.

What Goes in a Cybersecurity Portfolio?

A portfolio doesn't need to be flashy or complicated. It just needs to be real and accessible. Here's what it can include:

- **Projects and Code** – Host your scripts, automation tools, or lab write-ups on GitHub. Even a basic Python script that parses logs or port scans shows initiative.

- **CTF Walkthroughs** – Write up how you solved a challenge on TryHackMe or Hack The Box. Share what you tried, what worked, and what you learned.

- **Blog Posts or Short Write-Ups** – You don't need to be a writer. Just explain what you did and why it mattered. "Here's how I built my home lab" or "What I learned from analyzing a phishing email" is more than enough.

- **Screenshots and Lab Notes** – Document your journey. Save notes, screenshots, and summaries from your labs. These become valuable when you're talking through your experience in interviews.

- **Cybersecurity Checklist or Cheat Sheet** – Create a guide for small businesses, or your own CLI command cheat sheet. Not only does this help others, it shows that you're organizing knowledge in a practical way.

You Don't Need Permission

You don't need a job title to act like a cybersecurity professional. The work you're doing now—learning, building, testing, writing—that's the work that matters. Show it.

Use GitHub for code. Use Medium, Dev.to, or your own blog for write-ups. Post about your progress on LinkedIn. These small steps create visibility and tell a story: you're consistent, you're curious, and you're invested in this field.

And guess what? That's exactly what hiring managers want to see.

You're not trying to prove you're an expert—you're proving that you're serious. That you're coachable. That you're already doing the work.

That will opens doors.

Self-Paced or Structured?

Not everyone learns the same way—and that's okay.

Some people thrive with total freedom. They explore at their own pace, bounce between tools, and build their own systems as they go. Others need structure—clear milestones, deadlines, and a step-by-step plan. Neither approach is better. The key is figuring out what works best for you and then leaning into it.

If You're a Self-Paced Learner...

You're probably the type who likes flexibility and figuring things out on your own. You don't mind watching YouTube tutorials at midnight or tinkering in a lab for hours until something finally clicks.

Your toolkit might look like:

- TryHackMe or Hack The Box for hands-on learning

- YouTube channels like NetworkChuck or John Hammond

- GitHub to track and share your projects

- Books and blogs for deeper understanding

You'll need to stay organized. Use a notebook, spreadsheet, or Kanban board to track what you're learning and what you want to tackle next. It's easy to go down rabbit holes—fun but also distracting. Keep one eye on the goal.

If You Need Structure and Accountability...

You probably do better with a roadmap. You like knowing what's coming next and checking boxes as you move forward. That's awesome—structure keeps momentum going when motivation dips.

Your toolkit might include:

- Courses on Coursera, edX, or Udemy

- Certification programs like Google's or CompTIA's

- Bootcamps (free or paid) that offer live support or group projects

- Career path platforms like Cybrary or RangeForce

Set a study schedule. Join study groups. Use forums or Discord channels for accountability and motivation. You're not doing this alone—even if it feels that way sometimes.

Blend It If You Need To

Most people aren't purely one or the other. You might like the structure of a course during the week but enjoy going rogue in your lab on weekends. That's the sweet spot: use structure to build your foundation, then explore freely to apply and reinforce what you've learned.

There's no "one right way" to break into cybersecurity—only the way that keeps you consistent, curious, and moving forward.

Track Your Progress

Here's something no one talks about enough: cybersecurity learning can feel overwhelming—especially in the beginning. There's always more to study, more tools to try, more acronyms to Google. And because you're always chasing new knowledge, it's easy to forget how far you've come.

That's why tracking your progress is so important.

Why Tracking Matters

You might not feel like you're improving day to day, but over time? The results stack up. Keeping track of what you've learned helps you stay motivated, recognize growth, and build confidence.

It also gives you real data for your resume, your portfolio, and interviews. You'll be able to say more than "I learned some things." You'll be able to show exactly what you did, how you did it, and what impact it had.

Simple Ways to Track Your Learning

You don't need anything fancy. A spreadsheet, a Google Doc, or even a physical journal will work. Here are a few methods to consider:

Skills Journal

Write down what you worked on this week. What concept clicked? What tool did you explore? What challenge did you overcome? These short notes become a timeline of your growth.

Learning Roadmap

Break down your goals into steps. Want to pass Security+? Great—list the domains, track your study time, and log practice scores. Trying to build a SOC portfolio? Plan your lab setup, tools to learn, and small projects to complete.

Portfolio Tracker

For every project, CTF, or script you complete, jot down what it was, what you learned, what challenges you hit, and how you'd improve it next time. This turns random experiments into resume-ready talking points.

Celebrate Small Wins

Not everything has to be a massive accomplishment. Solved a challenge on TryHackMe? That's a win. Figured out a regex pattern that actually works? Huge win. Wrote your first Python script? Win. Survived your first failed lab attempt and tried again? That's one of the biggest wins.

Cybersecurity is full of small victories. Don't wait until you land a job to start celebrating. Recognizing these milestones builds momentum and reminds you that you're on the right path—even if it feels slow sometimes.

Keep showing up. Keep documenting. Keep improving.

You're Still Here? Good

If you've made it this far, you're already doing something most people never will: you're showing up for yourself. You're investing in your future. You're doing the work.

Breaking into cybersecurity isn't easy. There's confusion, gatekeeping, imposter syndrome, and job postings that ask for three years of experience for an "entry-level" role. It's frustrating. It's messy. It's exhausting.

Cybersecurity isn't one-size-fits-all. It needs defenders and hackers. Builders and auditors. Writers, educators, engineers, and analysts. Whether you're introverted or extroverted, technical or strategic, coming from tech or pivoting from something totally different—this field thrives on diverse backgrounds and different perspectives.

So don't wait until you "feel ready." That feeling may never come. You get ready by doing.

Keep showing up. Keep building. Keep asking questions. Keep failing forward.
Celebrate your small wins. Track your progress. Share your story.

No one can promise you a job. But if you stay consistent and focused, you will be too skilled, too valuable, and too persistent to ignore.

Turning Learning into Experience

Now that you know what to learn, how to learn it, and how to show it—there's still one big hurdle left: experience. How do you get real-world practice when nobody hires you without it?

That's exactly what the next chapter is about.

We'll explore how to gain meaningful experience—even without a job title—through labs, projects, volunteering, community work, and more. These are the things that move your resume from "potential" to "proven."

Let's get to it.

Chapter 4

Gaining Experience Without a Job

You've been learning the skills, knocking out labs, maybe earned a certification or two—you're building momentum.

But now comes the big question:
"How do I get experience if nobody will hire me without it?"

It's one of the most frustrating parts of breaking into cybersecurity. You see job listings for "entry-level" roles that still want one to three years of experience. And you're left wondering, *"How am I supposed to get that if no one gives me a shot?"*

Well, you can start gaining practical, relevant experience right now—on your own terms.

Experience isn't just about having a job title, it's about showing you can do the work. If you can solve problems, document your process, and explain what you've learned, that's experience. And that's exactly what hiring managers want.

Let's get to work.

The Experience Chicken-and-Egg Problem

Let's talk about the thing that makes most newcomers want to flip their desks.

You've been studying. Watching videos. Maybe passed Security+ or knocked out a few CTFs. You start browsing job boards—and boom:

"Entry-level role. Must have 1–3 years of experience."

Excuse me? How are you supposed to get experience if no one hires you without experience? This is the cybersecurity version of the chicken-and-egg problem. It's real. It's frustrating. And no, you're not imagining it. But honestly this common across the board no matter what type of job you're applying for.

But here's the part that many people don't realize: Experience doesn't just come from a job title.

It comes from doing the work. From building, breaking, fixing, documenting. Showing up and solving real problems—even if it's in your home lab or volunteer work.

You don't need a company to validate your skills. You just need proof that you're putting in the reps.

What Counts as Experience?

As stated before, experience isn't limited to job titles.

Sure, hiring managers list "one to three years of experience" on job postings, but what they're really looking for is evidence that you can do the work. That you understand the tools, the problems, and the process. And the good news is—you don't need a job in cybersecurity to start building that kind of credibility.

If you've completed a TryHackMe room, that counts. If you've written a basic Python script that automates a scan or filters logs, that counts. If you've helped a nonprofit set up two-factor authentication or reviewed their password policy, that counts too.

What matters is that you're applying what you've learned. You're solving problems, testing tools, breaking things, fixing them, and—most importantly—learning from the process. And if you can explain what you did and why you did it, that's experience. Plain and simple.

In fact, some of the best candidates I've seen weren't the ones with the fanciest job titles. They were the ones who could walk me through a home lab they built, explain how they spotted a brute-force login in a packet capture, or describe how they helped a local organization get more secure. That kind of initiative, follow-through, and problem-solving? It's gold.

So, if you've been doubting whether your work "counts," stop right there. It does. The work you're doing now—no matter where it's happening—is building your skillset and proving that you belong in this field.

You don't need someone to give you a title. You just need to start doing the work—and sharing what you've learned along the way.

Build Credibility Without a Job Title

This is where a lot of people get stuck. They think, "If I haven't been officially hired, I'm not legit." But that's just not true.

You don't need a title to build credibility in cybersecurity. What you need is proof that you're putting in the work—and you can start doing that right now.

Start building things. Share your progress. Learn in public. You don't have to wait until you feel "ready," because the act of doing is what gets you ready. Post your projects. Write about what you're learning. Reflect on your challenges and breakthroughs. Even if it feels small, it adds up.

The reality is, there are people in the industry with certs and titles who have never touched a packet capture or set up a virtual lab. If you've done those things—even in a home setup— you're already ahead. You're not just talking about cybersecurity. You're practicing it.

When you document what you're doing, you're building a track record. This will help build trust with hiring managers.

Build a Lab, Build Confidence

If you've been waiting for someone to give you permission to start doing real cybersecurity work? This is it. You don't need a fancy setup or a six-figure job title. What you need is a lab.

Your lab is where everything starts to click. It's where you'll connect the dots between the tools you're learning and how they're actually used. It's where you get to break things, fix them, and gain the kind of confidence that only comes from hands-on practice.

And no, it doesn't have to cost a dime. A basic lab setup could be as simple as installing VirtualBox or VMware Player on your computer and spinning up a few virtual machines. Start with Kali Linux for your security tools, Metasploit as your intentionally vulnerable target, Windows 10 for endpoint practice, and maybe Security Onion if you want to simulate a blue team environment. That's more than enough to get started with scanning, detection, hardening, scripting—you name it.

What makes a home lab so powerful is that you can try anything. You can experiment, make mistakes, and start over without consequences. Every time you troubleshoot an issue, write a script, or build out a scenario, you gain practical experience and become more confident.

And if your machine can't handle virtualization, no worries— cloud labs are a great alternative. Platforms like AWS, Azure, and Google Cloud offer free tiers that let you spin up servers, configure IAM policies, and simulate real-world environments. You'll learn how to lock down services, troubleshoot access issues, and build with security in mind—all in the same tools companies use every day.

Start somewhere. Pick a tool, build something, break it, and figure it out. Every hour in your lab is building more than just technical skills, it's building your confidence, and your experience. You're not waiting to be hired. You're already doing the work. Keep showing up.

Create Cybersecurity Projects

If you really want to stand out, especially when you don't have job experience yet—start building projects. Real, hands-on work you can point to and say, "Here's what I've done." Projects are more than practice. They give you something to showcase, something to talk about in interviews, and something that proves you can apply your skills in the real world.

And here's the best part: your projects don't need to be complex. In fact, the simple ones are often the most effective— because they solve real problems. Build a basic vulnerability scanner using Python and Nmap. Create a small SIEM dashboard with Splunk or ELK Stack and walk through how you'd use it during an investigation. If you're leaning toward GRC, draft a sample security policy based on NIST or ISO 27001 and explain how it would be implemented in a small business.

By doing these exercises you won't only be getting your technical reps, but you're also learning how to explain what you did—why you chose the tools, what challenges you faced, what worked, and what didn't. That kind of reflection is gold when you're in an interview or talking to a mentor. It shows you're thinking critically, not just copying tutorials.

Share what you do. Push your code to GitHub, post lessons learned on LinkedIn or write a short blog. Show that you're out here building, learning, and leveling up.

Capture the Flag (CTF) Challenges

CTFs are like interactive puzzles that teach you real-world hacking, analysis, and problem-solving techniques. Each challenge is designed to test and build your knowledge.

Break into a web app, decrypt a hidden message, reverse-engineer a small program, or hunt down suspicious behavior in a log file. Some challenges lean offensive (red team), others defensive (blue team), but all of them stretch your thinking and force you to learn by doing.

Don't worry if you've never done one before. You're not expected to be a hacker overnight. Start with beginner-friendly platforms like TryHackMe, which has guided learning paths and step-by-step walkthroughs. PicoCTF is another great one—created by Carnegie Mellon, it's designed specifically for people just getting started. If you're more defense-focused, check out CyberDefenders for blue team-oriented challenges.

What really makes CTFs valuable is how they train you to think. You start learning how attackers find weaknesses, how defenders detect them, and how both sides approach solving problems creatively. And when you finish a challenge—win or lose—write about it. Even a short recap of what you learned or what stumped you shows initiative and reflection.

CTFs don't just sharpen your skills—they give you real stories to tell. When someone asks, "Have you ever done any real-world analysis?" you can say, "Yeah, let me show you how I found and exploited a misconfigured login portal on a simulated network."

That's the kind of experience that separates you from the crowd.

Volunteer or Freelance

One of the most underrated ways to gain experience in cybersecurity is also one of the most rewarding: help someone.

Seriously. You don't need a job title to do real cybersecurity work. You just need to find a problem and offer to solve it.

Small businesses, nonprofits, schools, and community organizations often don't have the resources when it comes to cybersecurity. They don't have budgets for full-time cyber staff, and I wouldn't be surprised if they are using "password123" across the board. That's where you come in.

Maybe you help a church set up multi-factor authentication. Maybe you create a password policy for a local nonprofit. Maybe you volunteer to secure a school's cloud storage or teach a small business owner how to spot phishing emails. These might sound like small wins—but they're real-world problems and solving them is real experience.

And yes, this kind of work belongs on your resume. Just because you didn't get a paycheck doesn't mean it doesn't count. Be clear about what you did, what tools or frameworks you used, and what impact it had. That's what hiring managers care about.

Not sure where to start? Ask around. Reach out to places you already support or care about. Offer to help in a safe, limited way, something low-risk but high-impact. You can even write up a basic scope and offer to sign an NDA to show you're serious.

You can also explore more structured options. Sites like VolunteerMatch sometimes post cyber-related gigs. Groups like CyberPeace Corps and I Am The Cavalry work on security issues. And if you're into privacy, advocacy, or civil rights, there's a growing demand for cyber volunteers in those spaces too. Go make a difference. You'll learn a ton, build relationships, and walk away with experience that actually matters.

Create a Cyber Portfolio

Think of it like your personal proof-of-work. It shows potential employers—not just what you know—but what you've *done*.

You don't need a stack of certifications or a fancy background to create one. All you need is a place to collect the things you're already working on labs, scripts, CTF write-ups, volunteer work, personal projects. It doesn't have to be perfect. It just has to be real.

Finished a TryHackMe room? Write a short post about what you learned. Created a basic Python script to automate scanning or parsing logs? Put it on GitHub with a readme. Helped a local nonprofit set up MFA or improve their password policy? Document your process like you're explaining it to a hiring manager—because one day, you will be.

A good portfolio doesn't just list tools. It tells stories. What problem were you solving? What tools did you use? What did you learn? What would you do differently next time?

Your portfolio can live just about anywhere. GitHub is perfect for code. A Notion page, Medium blog, or even a free Wix site works great for write-ups and documentation. You don't need bells and whistles. You need clarity, consistency, and curiosity on display.

If someone looks at your portfolio, they should walk away with a clear sense of what you've done, how you think, and where you're headed. It's your chance to say, "I may not have the job title yet—but I'm already doing the work."

That's what makes people take notice.

Start Learning in Public

Social media has changed how we do business and can be a powerful tool to get you some exposer by learning in public.

That doesn't mean pretending to be an expert. It means sharing what you're learning *as you're learning it*. You don't need to wait until you've "made it" to start posting. In fact, it's more powerful when you don't.

Post about a lab you completed, the challenge you struggled with, or the tool you finally figured out. It does three things. One, it reinforces your learning. Two, it builds your confidence. And three, it shows others (including hiring managers) that you're consistent, curious, and serious about this field. Also, it gives you the opportunity to get some feedback from the community.

You're not just absorbing information. You're acting and reflecting on the process—and that stands out.

You don't need to post anything groundbreaking. A simple "Today I finished this TryHackMe room and learned how to spot open ports with Nmap" is enough. Share a screenshot, jot down a takeaway, explain what stumped you and how you got past it.

This is what people mean when they say *learn in public*. It's not about building an audience—it's about building momentum.

Post on LinkedIn, GitHub, X (formerly Twitter)—wherever feels comfortable. Use hashtags like #100DaysOfCyber, #BlueTeam, or #CyberSecurity to connect with others. You'll start to build a network without even realizing it. People will start to notice, peers, mentors, recruiters. You don't need to be perfect or polished. You just need to show up.

Network While You Learn

I get it, putting yourself out there and talking to people can be intimidating. And honestly, in my experience, a lot of folks in this field lean introverted. But here's the thing: networking can be a huge help when you're trying to get your foot in the door. Connecting with others while you're still figuring things out is actually one of the smartest things you can do. It often leads to opportunities that never show up on job boards.

Start small. Join InfoSec Prep, Cyber Mentor Academy, or Blue Team Village on Discord. These chat groups are full of beginners, seasoned pros, and mentors who've been exactly where you are. Reddit's got great communities too, like r/cybersecurity and r/netsecstudents, where you'll find advice, support, and real-talk feedback.

LinkedIn can be a game-changer. You don't need to post every day—just having a profile, following people in the field, and joining in on conversations can go a long way. Leave a comment, ask a question, or share something you're learning. That's how real connections start.

And when you're ready, check out local meetups or virtual conferences. Groups like OWASP, ISC2, and BSides often host free or low-cost events.

The biggest thing? Be honest about where you're at and where you're trying to go. You don't need to pretend to know everything. Just be curious, respectful, and open to learning. That mindset alone puts you ahead of the game.

From Practice to Confidence

Here's something you might not realize yet: every lab you finish, every tool you test, every challenge you push through, it's not just building your skills.

It builds your confidence.

Not the surface-level kind that comes from passing a cert or collecting likes on a LinkedIn post. I'm talking about *earned confidence*. The kind of confidence that comes from doing the work, solving real problems (even if they're in your home lab), and pushing through the messy middle when things don't make sense at first.

Confidence doesn't show up all at once. It shows up quietly—
when you troubleshoot a broken VM instead of giving up.
When you finally figure out what those log entries mean. When
you write a blog post even though you're still learning, and
someone messages you to say it helped them. That's growth.

You'll feel it most in interviews. Someone will ask, "Have you
worked with SIEM tools?" and instead of fumbling, you'll say,
"Yes, I've been using the free version of Splunk in my lab. I set
up log ingestion for a Windows VM and built some alerts to
track brute-force attempts."

You're not bluffing. You're not reciting theory. You're pulling
from *your actual experience*—because you put in the reps.

And that? That's what hiring managers remember. Not the
polished answers, but the real ones.

So, if you've been wondering, *"Am I good enough yet?"*—you're
asking the wrong question.

The real question is, *"Have I been doing the work?"*
If the answer is yes, then you're already further along than you
think.

Making the Leap to Your First Job

You've been learning. You've been building. You've been
showing up—even when it wasn't easy. And now, you've got
something most people never take the time to create: a body of
work that proves you're serious.

You've built skills. You've built experience. Now it's time to
turn all of that into opportunity.

If Chapter 4 was about proving it to yourself, Chapter 5 is about
proving it to the people who can hire you.

You've done the work. Now let's go get you a job.

Chapter 5

Landing Your First Cybersecurity Job

You've been working hard building skills, knocking out some projects, maybe even earning a cert or two. You've been putting in the hours, getting hands-on, and building real experience. Doesn't matter if your job title doesn't say "cybersecurity" yet—what matters is you're doing the work.

Now comes the next big step: Getting hired.

This chapter is all about helping you cross that bridge. I'm not here to give you the usual cookie-cutter advice like "just network more" or "apply to everything." That stuff doesn't work on its own. What I'm giving you here is practical, real-world strategy from someone who's done job hunting, sat on interview panels, and helped hired entry-level folks just like you.

Keep in mind you don't have to be perfect to land a job in cybersecurity. Nobody expects that. What you *do* need to show is that you're hungry to learn, willing to put in the effort, and be the kind of person others want to work with. That's what gets you in the door.

Let's break this down the right way—starting with the first move most people overlook: figuring out what kind of job you should actually be aiming for.

You're More Ready Than You Think

Let's start with this: if you've made it this far—through the studying, the labs, the projects, the certs—you're not "trying to break into cybersecurity" anymore.

You're already in.

The only thing standing between you and your first job is the next set of steps. You've already proven that you can learn, take initiative, and solve problems—three of the biggest things employers look for, no matter what the job title is.

Now, you might not feel fully ready. That's normal. Most people look at job listings and immediately count themselves out. "I don't have that skill." "I've never worked in a SOC." "They want three years of experience—I'm still learning." The self-doubt creeps in fast, even after you've done the work.

You don't need to check every box. Most of the time, neither does the person who gets the job. What makes you a strong candidate—especially in your first role, is that you've built a foundation and shown the potential to grow.

If you've been building a home lab, completing challenges on platforms like TryHackMe or Hack The Box, volunteering your skills, writing about your projects, or earning certifications—you already have experience. It may not come with a paycheck (yet), but it's real. And it counts.

Decoding Entry-Level Job Descriptions

If you haven't been scrolling through job boards let me go ahead and warn you that you will come across some strange post, like "entry-level" jobs not being very entry-level. You'll may see listings that say things like:

- "Entry-level SOC Analyst – 2 to 3 years experience required"

- "Junior Security Engineer – must be proficient in SIEM, scripting, AWS, and threat hunting"

- "Security Associate – CISSP preferred" (CISSP requires five years of experience, by the way.)

This kind of stuff is frustrating. And confusing. But here's what you need to know: most job descriptions are wish lists, not checklists. Hiring managers often load them up with every tool, skill, and cert they'd like in a perfect candidate—but they don't expect to find someone who hits every single one.

Your job is to read between the lines.

Start by figuring out which parts of the description are core requirements, and which ones are "nice to have." If they're asking for familiarity with networking concepts, basic security principles, log analysis, or endpoint protection—and you've been doing those things in your lab or training—that's your green light.

When it comes to the longer list of tools, platforms, or cloud environments, ask yourself: "Have I worked with something similar? Could I learn this quickly if I had to?" If the answer is yes, apply.

A good rule of thumb: if you meet 60–70% of the listed requirements and you're genuinely interested, go for it. Don't self-reject just because you don't check every box. Many hiring managers would rather hire someone eager to learn than someone who's technically qualified but unmotivated. If the job mentions Splunk, scripting, AWS, phishing simulations, or compliance frameworks, and you've touched any of those in your projects or labs, include them in your application.

Not every listing will be realistic. Some really are unicorn jobs disguised as entry-level roles. That's okay—just keep moving. The more you read, the better you'll get at spotting the difference between "we know what we need" and "we're not sure what we're hiring for."

And if in doubt? Apply anyway. Let them tell you no—you don't need to do it for them.

Building a Cyber-Ready Resume

Your resume is often your first real handshake with an employer. In cybersecurity, it doesn't need to be flashy or overly complicated—it just needs to be clear, focused, and proof that you can do the work. If you've been building labs, earning certifications, tackling CTFs, or working on personal projects, you already have experience that belongs on a resume. The key is organizing it in a way that highlights your skills and makes your growth obvious at a glance.

Start with a short, confident summary. This isn't the place to list everything you've ever done—it's your opening pitch. Keep it to two or three sentences that explain who you are, what you've been working on, and what kind of role you're aiming for. For example, someone might say they're an aspiring SOC Analyst with hands-on experience in threat detection, log analysis, and using tools like Splunk and Wireshark—all built through home lab projects and self-guided learning. That kind of summary immediately signals potential.

Next comes your skills section. Organize this into categories like tools and platforms, operating systems, scripting languages, and core security concepts. Think Splunk, Kali Linux, Python, PowerShell, the CIA triad, IAM—whatever you've actually used or studied. Keep focused on what's relevant to the jobs you're applying for.

One of the most important sections, especially for career changers or self-taught learners, is your project and lab experience. This is where you show your initiative. Treat these like job entries. Describe what you did, what tools you used, and what the outcome was. Something as simple as "Built and maintained a home lab simulating a SOC environment. Detected and documented brute-force attacks using Splunk and Windows Event Logs" tells a hiring manager a lot more than a generic bullet point ever could.

Certifications and education should follow. List the certs you've earned, the year, and skip "in progress" unless you're actively studying and close to completing. For education, include formal degrees if you have them—but don't discount the power of online courses, bootcamps, or self-paced study programs. Just be honest and specific.

Keep your resume to one page when you're starting out. You can always link to your GitHub, portfolio, or LinkedIn if someone wants to dig deeper. And be sure to use strong, clear language—action verbs like built, configured, analyzed, detected, documented, and secured go a long way. If you can quantify something, even better. "Completed 20+ labs on TryHackMe" or "Managed simulated alerts across three systems" adds weight.

If formatting stresses you out, lean on tools like Resumake, NovoResume, or FlowCV. They're free or low-cost, easy to use, and get the job done. Checkout resume example on next page.

JOHN SNOW

123-456-7891

jsnow@email.com

Somewhere, USA

LinkedIn.com/in/jsnow

PROFESSIONAL OVERVIEW

Detail-oriented IT support professional pivoting into cybersecurity, with strong experience in endpoint troubleshooting, user support, and system monitoring. Recently built a home SOC lab and completed over 30 hands-on security labs focused on threat detection, log analysis, and vulnerability scanning. Eager to bring my technical foundation and growing security skills into a Tier 1 SOC Analyst role.

WORK EXPERIENCE

IT Support Specialist

ABC Tech, City, State | 2022- Present

- Provided Tier 1 and Tier 2 support for 500+ end-users across hardware, software, and account access issues
- Administered Active Directory accounts, group policies, and permissions
- Monitored system health and event logs, escalating critical alerts and suspicious activities to sysadmin team

PROJECTS & LABS

Home SOC Lab

- Built a virtual SOC environment using Splunk, Kali Linux, and Windows
- Parsed Windows Event Logs to detect brute-force login attempts
- Created basic dashboards and alerts for account lockouts and system anomalies

TryHackMe & BTLO Labs

- Completed 30+ hands-on labs simulating attacks, detection, and mitigation strategies
- Documented findings in a personal GitHub repository
- Practiced log correlation, privilege escalation, and incident triage scenarios

EDUCATION

A.S., Cybersecurity and Information Assurance – *XYZ Community college, 2021*

SKILLS

- Splunk
- Wireshark
- Nessus
- Active Directory
- ATO/ATC
- Windows/Linux
- Even Log Analysis
- PowerShell
- IAM

CERTIFICATIONS

- CompTIA Security+
- Google Cybersecurity Certificate

Writing a Standout Cover Letter

A good cover letters can be a strong tool. It gives you the opportunity to go beyond the bullet points and show the human behind the resume. You can help connect the dots for a hiring manager and help you stand out, especially if you don't have a traditional background.

You don't need to write an essay. Three or four short paragraphs are plenty. And don't waste space with generic lines about being a "hard worker" or "team player." Focus on why you're excited about the role, what you've already done to prepare, and how your mindset and skills align with what they need.

If there's a specific reason you're applying to that company— maybe you admire their mission, you're familiar with the tools they use, or the role lines up perfectly with your goals—say that. Show them you've done your homework.

Then highlight the work you've done so far. Mention your home lab, your volunteer efforts, your certs, or a specific project relevant to the position. Even if you haven't had a paid cybersecurity role, you can absolutely talk about what you've built and what you've learned.

Finally, close strong. Make it clear that while you're still early in your cybersecurity journey, you're serious, coachable, and ready to grow. Here's a simple example that hits all the right notes:

Dear [Hiring Manager],

I'm excited to apply for the Junior SOC Analyst role at [Company Name]. I've been following your team's work in threat detection and love how you approach cybersecurity with a focus on continuous improvement.

Over the past year, I've built a home lab where I've practiced log analysis, created detection rules in Splunk, and responded to simulated brute-force attacks. I've also completed the CompTIA Security+ certification and regularly participate in TryHackMe and CyberDefenders challenges.

While I'm early in my cybersecurity career, I've proven I can learn fast, solve problems, and take initiative. I'm looking for a team where I can grow, contribute, and continue sharpening my skills—and I believe [Company Name] is that place.

Thank you for considering my application. I'd love the chance to talk more about how I can support your team.

Sincerely,
[Your Name]

Keep it real. Keep it focused. And don't be afraid to show genuine excitement about the opportunity. Hiring managers notice that.

Where to Find Entry-Level Cyber Jobs

Knowing where to look can save you hours of frustration. There are more cybersecurity roles than ever, but not all of them are easy to find—especially at the entry level. Some are buried in generic IT job boards, others are tucked away on niche platforms, and a lot of the best ones are never publicly posted at all.

Start with the familiar platforms:

- **LinkedIn** is probably the strongest for cybersecurity because it combines job listings with networking. You can find junior and contract roles, follow companies, and connect with recruiters in one place.
- **Indeed** is still solid, especially with filters for experience level and location.
- **Dice** leans more tech-heavy and is worth checking if you've got an IT background.
- **ClearanceJobs** is essential if you have (or are aiming for) a U.S. security clearance.

But don't stop there. Look for opportunities at MSPs—Managed Service Providers that handle IT and security for small businesses. These are often overlooked gold mines for learning fast and wearing many hats. Check local tech firms, startups, and even university IT departments. You might be surprised how many places need security support but don't advertise with a "cyber" job title.

Security vendors—think companies that make antivirus software, SIEM tools, or cloud security platforms—are also worth a look. Many have entry-level support or analyst roles that aren't front-facing but are perfect for learning from the inside.

And while job boards matter, sometimes the best leads come from people. Start connecting with recruiters who specialize in cybersecurity. Follow hiring managers at companies you admire. Attend virtual conferences, job fairs, or Capture the Flag competitions—these often include career booths and real hiring opportunities you won't see elsewhere.

The key is not to apply everywhere. Apply where you actually fit—and where your effort has the best chance of paying off. A focused search will always beat a scattered one.

Applying Strategically

One of the most common mistakes people make is mass applying. You start scrolling through listings, and for every position titled "Cybersecurity Analyst" you submit a generic application—no customization, no focus, just hoping something sticks.

I understand you are eager to get your foot in the door, but spray-and-pray isn't the best strategy to land a job in cyber. I know I said there is a huge shortage of cybersecurity professionals, that doesn't many companies are just hiring anyone that applies. Hiring managers can spot a copy-paste resume from a mile away. If you really want to stand out, you need to slow down and apply with purpose.

Instead of sending out dozens of resumes, focus on a handful of roles that actually align with your skills and interests. Read the job descriptions carefully. Look for the keywords—tools, platforms, core responsibilities—and mirror that language in your resume and cover letter. You could even use tools like ChatGPT to help.

Even if it takes more time, this targeted approach gets better results. One strong application is worth more than fifty that doesn't say anything meaningful.

Keep track of roles you apply for on a spreadsheet. Write down the company name, the date you applied, and which version of your resume you used. Add notes about any recruiters or people you connected with related to the role. Keeping yourself organized like this makes it easier to stay on top of the process and avoid mistakes like applying twice.

While applying is important, sometimes finding someone working in a role you're interested in and asking if they'd be open to a quick conversation about the role can help you better prepare, networking is a powerful tool. A simple message asking about their career path, their day-to-day responsibilities, or any advice they'd give someone getting started can go a long way.

These often called informational interviews—might not lead to a job offer right away, but they can lead to insights, mentorship, and even referrals. Just be respectful of people's time, be clear about your intentions, and follow up with gratitude.

Interview Prep

Nothing like a job interview to get you second guessing everything you have learned. Even after building labs, writing scripts, earning certs, and completing courses, imposter syndrome has a way of creeping in right before you hit "Join Meeting." That's normal. All you need to do is remind yourself you've already done more than most people even attempt. This is just the part where you learn how to talk about it.

The interview isn't about being perfect. It's about showing that you're coachable, resourceful, and able to think through problems under pressure. If you've been learning hands-on, building projects, and documenting what you've done, then you're already a stronger candidate than you realize.

For the most part interviews will consist of a mix of technical and situational questions. The technical questions aren't meant to test deep expertise—they're meant to confirm you've got a grasp of the fundamentals. Expect questions like: What's the difference between a threat and a vulnerability? What does the CIA triad stand for? How would you identify a suspicious login attempt in a log file? They may also ask how you stay current on cybersecurity trends, or what tools you've worked with—especially if they're listed in the job description. Don't worry about having the perfect answer. If you're unsure, be honest. Say something like, "That's something I'm still learning, but here's how I'd approach it." Employers respect honesty and curiosity a lot more than guessing and trying to bluff your way through.

Situational questions are about how you work with people and how you handle challenges. You'll hear things like, "Tell me about a time you solved a difficult problem," or "How do you handle pressure?" or "Give an example of how you learned something quickly." Use real-life examples from your lab work, training, or volunteer experience, these count. Talk about the time you set up a SIEM in your home lab and had to troubleshoot bad data feeds? That's a story. That phishing awareness presentation you gave at the library to the public? That's relevant. Structure your answers using the STAR method—Situation, Task, Action, Result—to keep things organized and focused.

Preparation is key. You don't need to memorize answers, but you should be familiar with your own experience. Go back over your labs, your GitHub repos, your notes. Practice by talking to yourself in a mirror or doing mock interviews with a friend. It'll feel awkward at first, but it's one of the best ways to build confidence.

Virtual interviews are now common place in the hiring process, don't get caught off guard. Most first-round interviews happen on Zoom or Teams these days. Make sure you have a working camera and mic, pick a quiet room in your house, and clean up your desktop in case you're asked to share anything. Make sure you have good lighting, last thing you want is to look like a gremlin in a dark cave. An easy hack for lighting is to sit facing a window. Also Dress professionally. It might feel weird, but it helps set the tone. Keep a printed or digital copy of your resume, job description, and any notes nearby just in case.

Finally, follow up by sending a short thank-you email afterward. Just thank them for their time and let them know you're excited about the opportunity. This is more than enough to make a strong impression.

Handling Rejections and Staying Motivated

You got the interview, but you didn't get the job, rejection can suck but it is an opportunity to learn. You're going to hear "no" a few times. Maybe more than a few. Thats' ok.

It doesn't mean you're not good enough. It doesn't mean you've failed. It means you're in the game.

Rejection is part of the process. It happens to everyone—even me with years of experience, multiple certs, and a polished résumé. There are multiple reasons why you didn't get the job. Timing, internal referrals, role gets put on hold, or yes someone did better than you did on the interview. Don't take it personally.

It stings I get it. Here's how to handle it and keep your momentum.

First, don't take it as a sign to stop. Every interview, every application, every connection is experience gained. You're building stamina, sharpening your communication skills, and learning how to navigate the hiring process. Every "no" brings you closer to a "yes."

If you make it to an interview and don't get the job, try to follow up. A short email asking for feedback—just a sentence or two—is often appreciated. The feedback provided is gold, use it to adjust and improve.

Second, This isn't about landing just any job—it's about building a career. There will be hard days. You'll question if you're doing enough, if you're behind, if you're even cut out for this. That's normal. It's important to keep pushing forward.

Third, play the long game. This field needs people that are determined, curious, and willing to learn. You might not land the first job you apply for or ten. But if you stay consistent and keep improving, it *will* happen.

Consistency pays off. It's not about being the smartest. It's about showing up, doing the work, and refusing to quit when it gets hard.

You only need one yes. Keep going until you get it.

Thriving in Your First Cyber Job

So far, you've studied the landscape, built hands-on skills, created a personal roadmap, started applying with purpose, and learned how to navigate interviews and setbacks like a pro.

That's not just preparation—that's momentum.

But landing the job? That's just the beginning.

Your first cybersecurity role is where the real learning kicks in. You'll be surrounded by new tools, new people, new pressures—and new opportunities to grow. It might feel overwhelming at first, and that's okay. No one expects you to know everything on day one. What matters is how you show up, how you contribute, and how you keep building from here.

In the next chapter, we'll talk about what it takes to not just survive but thrive in your first cybersecurity job. You'll learn how to make an impact early, work well with your team, manage imposter syndrome, and keep growing your skill set without burning out.

You've earned your shot. Now it's time to make it count.

Let's go.

Chapter 6

Thriving in Your First Cybersecurity Job

You Got The Job, Now What?

This is where the real fun begins. You're finally inside the world you've been working so hard to break into. But even with the offer letter signed and the onboarding paperwork out of the way, it's totally normal to feel nervous. You might be wondering, "Am I actually ready for this?" Or worse, "What if they find out I'm not as good as they think?"

These types of thoughts are common in high demand jobs not only in cybersecurity, Imposter Syndrome. Don't worry, it's not a red flag. The important thing to understand is this: you're not expected to know everything. What you are expected to do is learn, grow, ask smart questions, and keep showing up.

During your first few months on the job don't worry about proving you are an expert in the field, nobody expects you to be especially if this is your first cyber role. You need to focus on listening, observing, absorbing the way your team works, and aligning yourself with how they handle threats, policies, tools, and communication. This chapter is your guide to not just surviving your first job—but thriving in it.

We'll talk about how to navigate your first 90 days, build strong habits, make yourself a valuable teammate, and keep your learning momentum going even after you've got that title. You'll see what different roles look like day to day, how to continue leveling up on the job, and how to manage stress in a field that doesn't always slow down.

This isn't about having all the answers. It's about asking the right ones, learning how to learn, and building a career that grows with you. You've worked hard to get here. Now let's make it count.

Welcome to the Team

You made it. You're officially on the inside—badge, email address, Slack login, and all. Maybe you're joining a SOC, a GRC team, a security vendor, or supporting a compliance function inside a larger company. Either way, your first cybersecurity job is here... and now you're asking, "What do I actually do now?"

First, take a breath. It's completely normal to feel overwhelmed, as I mentioned before Imposter syndrome is a very real thing, you just can't let it take control or else it will hold you back and stunt your growth.

In the early weeks on the job you're not expected to move mountains in most cases. I say most cases since not all leadership is the same, so like any job be prepared to deal and handle bad bosses.

With that said, for the most part you will be expected to observe, absorb, and align. Watch how the team operates. Learn the flow of communication. Get a feel for the tools, the terminology, and the priorities. Ask good questions. It's important to take the time to understand the business—not just the security side, but how everything connects. At the end of the day all businesses care about one thing "how does this save me money".

This is your foundation. The stronger you make it, the more confident you'll feel when it's time to contribute. So don't worry about impressing anyone on day one. Focus on learning the ropes, being coachable, and showing up with the same work ethic that got you hired in the first place.

The real growth starts here.

Mastering the First 90 Days

Think of your first 90 days like joining Voltron.

You're not just another pilot, you're part of something bigger. When you land on the team, you shouldn't start swinging a sword solo. This is your time to figure out: Who's already here? How do they operate? Are you the leg, the arm, or maybe the head? Because while each lion can handle themselves in a fight, Voltron is strongest when everyone moves together coordinated, aligned, and trusting each other. That's your mission in the early days: learn the system, build trust, and earn your place in the formation.

Start by understanding the company's mission and how your role in security supports it. Whether you're in a SOC, compliance, GRC, or AppSec, you're one part of a larger machine. Ask yourself: What's critical to business? Who depends on your work? What threats keep leadership up at night? These questions help you sync your actions with what matters—not just what looks flashy.

Then, get hands-on with the tools. Learn the stack—SIEMs like Splunk or Sentinel, ticketing systems, endpoint protection, whatever's in play. But don't stop at the button clicking. Understand how each "lion" contributes to the fight. Why were this tools chosen? What's its blind spot? What does normal look like—and how can you tell when it's not?

One of your best early moves? Find your fellow pilots. There's always someone who's the go-to for technical deep dives, someone who understands policy inside out, and someone who can give you historical context for why things are the way they are. Lean on your team members. Learn from them. Let them help you navigate the terrain.

I recommend keeping a journal to take notes. Whether it's Notion, a Google Doc, or a beat-up green book, start capturing what you're learning: tools, acronyms, escalation paths, login info, tribal knowledge. This will be your personal cockpit manual when the pressures on.

And above all—ask questions. Curiosity shows you care. It shows you're engaged. No one expects you to know everything out of the gate, but they will notice if you're listening, learning, and connecting the dots.

The first 90 days are your runway. Use them to sync up with the team, find your rhythm, and show you're ready to Voltron up when the time comes.

Habits of a Great Cybersecurity Professional

Certain habits set you apart from day one. These aren't just technical skills I'm talking about. These habits are the day-to-day behaviors that will earn you trust, build you a reputation of reliability, and quietly open doors over time.

First, get used to being detail oriented. In cybersecurity, small mistakes can cause major issues. Attention to detail can make or break how effective you are. Skipping a log entry or leaving out documentation might not seem like a big deal at the time. But when an audit happens or a security incident escalates, that missing information can quickly become critical.

And if it leads back to you, it won't reflect well. These kinds of details build your reputation—either as someone who's reliable or someone who cuts corners. Taking a few extra minutes now can save a lot of headaches later.

Second, stay calm under pressure. I can promise you incidents will happen, if they didn't, I wouldn't have a job. You might get a bunch of alerts at the same time. Deadlines can go from three weeks out to one week. I've had situations where projects have been on hold for months and randomly come back on and clients want deliverables within days. There will be times when you'll be the person expected to respond and come up with a game plan. The people who rise in this field are the ones who can keep a cool head, work through the problem step-by-step, and avoid panicking when things get noisy. It's important to keep your cool and stay focused, the last thing you want to do is make avoidable mistakes.

Communication is another superpower. The ability to clearly explain what you're seeing—whether in a Slack message, a ticket, a report, or a meeting—is what turns technical work into team results. Learn how to communicate up and down the chain. That means being able to explain technical details to non-technical folks and also knowing how to brief your team lead with just the right amount of context. Clear communication builds trust and trust builds influence.

And finally, never stop learning, new threats emerge every day, tools change, regulations shift. The best people in this space are always studying, always experimenting, always asking, "What's next?" That doesn't mean you need to be in a course 24/7. Rather, be more like a cybersecurity Batman, "Expect the unexpected."

These habits won't show up on a certification or degree. But they're what separate the people who just have a job from the ones who build long, successful careers. Be the one people know they can count on—and the rest tends to follow.

Daily Life in Cybersecurity (Varies by Role)

One of the most interesting things about cybersecurity is how wildly different your day-to-day life can look depending on your role. You could be analyzing suspicious traffic, drafting policies, launching phishing simulations, or writing exploit code. It all depends on your path—and that's what makes this field so flexible.

Security Operations Center (SOC)- your day will likely revolve around triaging alerts. You'll monitor dashboards, review logs, and investigate anything that looks out of the ordinary. You'll probably start your shift checking for overnight incidents or reviewing tickets escalated by junior analysts. When an alert comes in—say, a strange login at 2 a.m. from a foreign IP—you'll dig into it. Is it a false positive? A compromised credential? You'll need to follow the trail, document your findings, and escalate if necessary. It's fast-paced, repetitive at times, but always full of learning.

GRC (Governance, Risk, and Compliance)- your days look completely different. You might be reviewing policy documents, assessing system risk, or mapping security controls to a standard like NIST. You may prepare for an audit or update your organization's incident response plan. There's less firefighting and more strategic thinking. If you're detail-oriented and enjoy the process, this might be your sweet spot.

Penetration testers- live in a whole different rhythm. Their time is split between reconnaissance, exploiting vulnerabilities, and reporting findings. You'll spend hours poking at systems, digging into misconfigurations, running tools like Burp Suite or Nmap—and then translating that into plain-English reports for stakeholders. Some days are exciting. Others involve testing one application for hours with no real results. But if you love puzzles and trying to think like an attacker, it's a rewarding path.

Security awareness or Training - you might spend time designing phishing campaigns, writing blog posts for internal teams, or building interactive training modules. Your goal is to improve behavior—get people thinking before they click, reporting suspicious activity, and following secure practices. It's part education, part psychology, and all about making cybersecurity human.

No matter what role you land in, here's one thing that's true across the board: no two days are exactly the same. There will be curveballs—unplanned incidents, surprise audits, urgent vulnerabilities. Some days you'll feel like you have a handle on everything. Other days, you'll feel like you're scrambling to keep up.

That's cybersecurity. And that's what makes it such a dynamic, never-boring career.

Being a Team Asset

In every cybersecurity team, there's someone people naturally turn to when they need help, clarity, or a quick answer. They may not have the most senior title, but they've earned trust— and they make the team stronger just by being there. Becoming that kind of person isn't about knowing everything. It's about how you show up.

One of the easiest ways to stand out early is to take the initiative. You don't have to wait for someone to hand you a big project. Look for small things that make life easier for your team. Maybe it's writing up a quick guide for a tool you just learned. Maybe it's cleaning up documentation that hasn't been touched in years. Maybe it's automating a repetitive task that slows everyone down. Little wins like that don't go unnoticed.

Ask how you can add value. Instead of just sitting around when you complete your own tasks, start thinking about what problems you can help solve. Is there a process that seems overly complicated that can be simplified? or A teammate who's overwhelmed? Offering to help—even in small ways— builds trust fast.

Another smart move is volunteering for unglamorous tasks. Take notes during a team meeting. Offer to start clearing out backlogs or build meeting slides. Or maybe you enjoy doing these types of task, If so good on you, should make it easier. When you're the one making everyone's work easier, people remember that.

Being a go-to person isn't always about having the answer. It's about being dependable, proactive, and helpful. When people know they can count on you—whether it's for clean documentation, a second pair of eyes on an alert, or just a level-headed opinion during a chaotic moment—you become someone they want on their team.

That kind of trust is hard to teach. But it's easy to earn—one small action at a time.

Continue Building Your Skills

Just because you landed the job doesn't mean you stop learning. In fact, now is when things really start to click. The best cybersecurity professionals treat every role—no matter how entry-level—as a platform to grow from. You're surrounded by real tools, real incidents, and real people with knowledge you can absorb. Don't let that go to waste.

Start by setting a few goals for yourself. Nothing too complicated—just a simple 3-, 6-, and 12-month learning roadmap. Ask yourself: What do I want to get better at? What tools do I want to master? What areas am I curious about but haven't explored yet? Maybe you want to dive deeper into SIEM queries, get better at report writing, or shadow the red team for a week. Write it down, check in with yourself regularly, and share those goals with your manager. Most leaders love to see that kind of initiative.

Next, identify one area you'd like to specialize in. It doesn't mean you're locked into it forever, but having a focus gives your growth some direction. Maybe you're drawn to threat hunting, cloud security, governance and policy, or endpoint hardening. Whatever it is, start leaning into it. Find out who the experts are on your team and ask for advice or guidance. Review their tickets. Ask them how they think through problems. Offer to help with documentation or testing. You'd be surprised how much people are willing to teach if you show genuine interest.

Also, don't isolate your learning to just your workplace. Stay active in the broader community. Keep following blogs, newsletters, and podcasts. Attend meetups, even virtually.

You don't have to move mountains every week. You just have to keep moving. One skill, one tool, one question at a time.

Stay Sharp After You Land the Job

At this point you might be wondering, "Do I still need more certifications?" hey, you already have the job right. The short answer? Maybe. Certs should support your growth, not become a never-ending checklist.

You don't need to grab every shiny badge just because you overheard someone hyping it up. Instead, start by looking at where you want to go in the next year or two—and then work backward. Let your job guide your learning. If you're in a SOC role and using a SIEM every day, it makes sense to pursue something like the CompTIA CySA+ or Splunk Core Certified User. If you're doing policy work or risk assessments, look into ISO 27001 Foundations, CISA, or CRISC down the road.

For pen testers, there's a natural progression too. You might start with something like eJPT—hands-on and beginner-friendly—and then work your way toward OSCP when you're ready for the more advanced material. If you're working in cloud environments, certifications like AWS Security Specialty or Azure Security Engineer Associate can not only sharpen your skills but also signal your focus to future employers.

The good news? A lot of companies are willing to pay for your certifications and training, especially if it directly benefits the work you're doing. Look in your employee handbook for "certification reimbursement" Don't be afraid to ask. Frame it as a way to bring more value to the team. Some companies even have training budgets or partner discounts through vendors like SANS, ISC2, or CompTIA. Use them.

As I have said before in this book, certs are tools, not trophies. A certification should backup your experience or prepare for your next role. If it doesn't do any of those things, it might not be worth your time or money right now.

Focus on the certs that move you forward—not the ones that just pad your resume.

Dealing with Burnout & Stress

I won't sugarcoat it, cybersecurity can be very stressful, some roles more than others. There are days when the alerts won't stop, your inbox is a mess, and a compliance deadline or security incident blows up your perfectly planned schedule. It's a field that moves fast, expects a lot, and doesn't always give you time to catch your breath. And if you're not careful, that pressure can pile up and burn you out before you even hit your stride.

The good news is, burnout isn't inevitable. But you do have to be intentional about managing your energy—just like you manage your time or tasks.

Start by recognizing that stress is part of the job, but chronic overwhelm shouldn't be. If you're consistently dreading Mondays or feeling like you're one bad day away from quitting, that's not something to just "tough out." That's a sign to take a step back and take a breath.

Build in small recovery windows. Even a 10-minute walk, a screen break, or an afternoon off can help reset your focus. If there is one thing I love to do it's hitting the gym after a stressful day but if working out isn't for you, try playing music, reading, gaming—whatever gets your mind off work is valid. It's not "wasting time"—it's maintenance.

Talk to your manager if things are getting out of hand. A good leader will want to know if the workload is unsustainable, if you're buried in noise, or if you're constantly being pulled in too many directions. Burned-out employees don't make secure environments. You're not being weak by speaking up, you're being responsible.

It also helps to find peers you can vent to. A check-in with a mentor or really anyone who is willing to listen, just getting the words out can really help.

Give yourself some props. You're learning, you're growing, and you're dealing with real problems in real-time. That's not easy. If you're here, showing up and doing your best, you're already doing more than enough.

Protect your mind like you protect your systems—because you're the most valuable asset in this equation.

Planning Your Long-Term Career Path

By now, you're past your foot being in the door. You're building skills, gaining experience, and starting to see what this world really looks like from the inside. That alone puts you ahead of most people who never take the leap. But once the dust settles and you've found your rhythm, it's natural to start wondering: *What's next?*

It's time to think long-term.

You don't need a five-year comprehensive plan mapped down to the job title. But it helps to think in short blocks—maybe 18 to 24 months at a time. Ask yourself: What do I want to be better at a year from now? What kind of problems do I want to be solving? What role or specialty am I starting to gravitate toward? Use your answers to guide your learning, your certifications, and your conversations with mentors or managers.

Sometimes growth means leveling up in the same track—going from SOC Analyst to Incident Responder to Threat Hunter. Other times, it means making lateral moves that expand your knowledge. You might go from compliance to cloud, or from red team to security architecture. These kinds of shifts don't mean you're starting over—it means you're building range, getting experience in multiple branches of cybersecurity will only make you a better cyber professional.

Keep revisiting your goals. Your interests will evolve. So will the industry. The field you entered won't be the same five years from now, and that's part of what makes it so exciting. Stay flexible.

And remember, your career path doesn't have to look like anyone else's. Some people rise fast, others build slow. Some go deep into technical work; others move toward strategy and leadership. The path you choose doesn't matter as long as you make it yours and just keep moving forward.

Growing Your Brand in Cybersecurity

By now, you've done what most people only talk about. You got in, you learned the ropes, and you started building real experience. You've faced the nerves of your first few months, asked the hard questions, made progress, and probably stumbled once or twice—but kept going anyway. That's what thriving looks like.

Now it's time to think bigger.

As you grow in this field, you'll start to realize that building your reputation, your *personal brand*—can be just as powerful as building your technical skills. It's what opens doors to opportunities you didn't even know existed: job offers, speaking engagements, mentorships, collaborations, maybe even starting something of your own one day.

You don't need to be an influencer. You just need to be *visible* and intentional about how you show up in the cybersecurity space. Whether it's sharing what you've learned, contributing to the community, or documenting your journey—your voice matters.

In the next chapter, we'll talk about how to build your professional presence, grow your network, and position yourself as someone worth knowing in this industry. In all business a lot of times it is who you know, not what you know that makes the difference. When the right people know what you bring to the table, the right opportunities tend to follow.

Let's make sure they see you.

Chapter 7

Growing Your Brand in Cybersecurity

At this point, you're learning, contributing, and building real skills. That alone puts you ahead of the crowd. But skills aren't the whole picture. Visibility matters too.

This chapter isn't about chasing likes or becoming an influencer. It's about making sure people know what you're capable of. Because in cybersecurity, opportunities often come through relationships—not résumés.

Most jobs in this field are filled through networks. A recruiter sees your LinkedIn post. A peer mentions your name in a meeting. Someone you chatted with in a Discord group drops your name when a role opens. These moments don't happen by chance. They happen when your name is already familiar.

That's what personal branding is, showing people what you're learning, what you care about, and how you think. Work your way to becoming an expert in your lane. Be consistent and real.

Let's walk through how to build your brand from the ground up.

Why Personal Branding Matters

In cybersecurity, it's easy to think the only thing that matters is your technical ability. But even in a technical field, trust and reputation still drive hiring decisions.

A personal brand builds that trust before you're even in the room. When someone sees your posts, reads your blog, or watches a walkthrough you recorded, they start to understand who you are and how you think. That familiarity matters. People hire who they know—or who they feel like they know.

Some may say LinkedIn is fading. But it still works, and many recruiters still use it. Your content can spark a conversation that leads to the right role. You don't need to be flashy. You just need to be consistent.

Build Your Cybersecurity Presence

LinkedIn is your résumé that doesn't sleep. It works in the background, letting recruiters and peers find you without you applying for anything.

Start with your headline. Avoid generic terms like "Job Seeker." Be specific. Use titles, tools, or certifications that show your focus. Something like "SOC Analyst | Security+ | Splunk | Cybersecurity Learner" gives a clearer picture.

Update your banner with something that reflects your interests. It doesn't have to be fancy—just relevant. Canva has templates that make this easy.

In your About section, tell your story. Where did you start? What are you learning? What interests you about cybersecurity? Keep it brief, honest, and human.

In Experience, don't just list jobs. Add internships, volunteer work, and even roles outside the field if they gave you useful skills. If you worked retail and handled sensitive customer info, that counts. Explain what you did and what you learned.

Add certifications and relevant training—even free courses. Then list your technical skills: Python, Splunk, log analysis, threat modeling, and others. These keywords help recruiters find you.

Once your profile is up to date, stay active. Comment on posts. Share what you're learning. One or two updates a week builds visibility.

Start Sharing Your Journey Publicly

You don't need to be an expert to post online. You just need to be learning—and willing to share.

A short recap of a TryHackMe room, a lab you finished, or a mistake you learned from can go a long way. It shows that you're engaged and reflective.

Try writing a short post after you complete a challenge. Share what you learned and how you approached the problem. Or explain a concept in your own words. Break down the CIA Triad or multi-factor authentication.

Curate helpful content too. If you find good blogs, tools, or resources, share them. That helps others and shows you're actively exploring.

Start with one post per week. Don't worry about perfect writing or polished formatting. The goal is to be consistent, not flawless.

Build a Simple Portfolio or Personal Site

A portfolio shows your work. It proves that you're not just learning, you're applying what you've learned.

Start with a short About Me section. Use parts of your LinkedIn summary. Say who you are, what you're learning, and what kind of work interests you.

Then highlight a few projects. These don't need to be large or advanced. A home lab, a phishing simulation, a dashboard you built, or a TryHackMe walkthrough all work. Add screenshots and write a short explanation: what problem you solved, what tools you used, and what you learned.

Link to your GitHub if you're writing scripts or documenting your work. Even simple projects show how you think.

Include your résumé, certifications, and contact info. Keep the layout simple and clean. Use GitHub Pages, Notion, Carrd, or any tool you're comfortable with. The design doesn't matter as much as the content.

Once it's live, link it in your résumé and LinkedIn profile.

Engage in Cyber Communities

You don't have to do this journey alone. In fact, one of the fastest ways to grow in cybersecurity—both in skills and in confidence—is to plug into the community. Whether it's Discord, LinkedIn, Reddit, or local meetups, being part of the conversation gives you exposure, support, and opportunities you can't get from studying in isolation.

Start with LinkedIn. Many cybersecurity professionals share ideas, tools, challenges, and wins. Engage with these folks, leave thoughtful comments, ask questions, react to posts from people in roles you're interested in. These small interactions are how relationships start. Over time, those relationships can turn into referrals, collaborations, or even mentorship.

Discord is another goldmine. Communities like InfoSec Prep, TryHackMe's official server, Blue Team Village, and others are packed with people learning exactly what you're learning. You'll find help on tools, career advice, accountability partners, and sometimes even job leads. The vibe is usually friendly, helpful, and welcoming to beginners.

If you're on Twitter (or X), follow thought leaders in your niche. Blue teamers, red teamers, GRC pros, and cloud security folks all have a presence there. It's where breaking news happens, tools get shared, and side conversations turn into valuable insights. You don't need to post all the time—just being part of the ecosystem keeps you in the loop.

Reddit can be surprisingly helpful too. Subreddits like r/cybersecurity, r/netsecstudents, and r/blueteamsec are full of learning threads, career questions, and tool breakdowns. Just take things with a grain of salt—Reddit is a mixed bag, so trust but verify.

And don't forget local or virtual meetups. OWASP chapters, BSides events, and DEF CON groups are great places to meet others who care about security, learn something new, and maybe even get some face time with local recruiters or employers. If you're not near a big city, many of these events stream online now—so there's no excuse not to show up.

The bottom line is this: community accelerates growth. You'll stay motivated, learn faster, and build relationships that pay off in ways you can't always predict. Don't wait until you "know enough" to join in. You belong in the room now. Pull up a chair.

Teach, Mentor, and Give Back

At some point, you'll realize you have something worth teaching. That doesn't mean you need a podcast or YouTube channel. It means your voice can help someone else.

Write a blog post about how you solved a lab. Record a simple walkthrough. Speak at a local event or online meetup. Just explain what you did, what went wrong, and what you figured out.

That's what I'm doing with this book. I've mentored soldiers, students, and junior analysts. I built a blog (cybtrps.com/cyber-blog) to reach more people. This book is another step.

When you teach, you grow. You solidify your knowledge. You gain confidence. And you help build the community that supports you.

Grow a Reputation Before You Need It

Don't wait to build your reputation. Do it now—before you're job hunting.

Reputation in cybersecurity carries weight. This field runs on trust. People remember who shows up, contributes, and helps others.

You don't need a big audience. You need to be consistent. One post. One comment. One conversation at a time.

Over time, your name starts to come up. A recruiter reaches out. A speaker slot opens up. A hiring manager sends a DM. You didn't pitch anyone, they found you.

Reputation isn't flashy. It's steady. It builds slowly but pays off when you need it most.

Keep Leveling Up — Consistently

The truth is, there's no finish line in cybersecurity—and that's a good thing. You'll never know it all. You'll never be "done." But you will keep leveling up, one project, one connection, one challenge at a time.

The key is consistency, not intensity. You don't need to study ten hours a day, post every morning, or launch a new project every week. You just need to keep showing up—learning, contributing, and pushing yourself a little further each quarter.

One simple way to track your growth? Reflect every few months. What did you learn? What did you build? Who did you connect with? What skills or certs did you add? Treat your career like a living document. Update your résumé, refresh your portfolio, and take stock of how far you've come.

And when you've mastered something? Teach it. Share what you've learned in a post, a blog, a video, or a conversation with someone who's just getting started. Teaching is how you solidify your own knowledge—and how you become a valuable part of the community that helps you.

Your brand, your network, and your body of work are long-term assets. They'll grow with you, reflect your journey, and open doors you didn't even know were there. But only if you keep building them, one step at a time.

Pace yourself. Stay hungry. Stay grounded. And keep moving forward.

Long-Term Career Growth in Cybersecurity

You've broken in. You've built skills and started showing the world what you're about. That's a major milestone.

Next, we'll talk about how to keep that momentum. How to move into leadership, find your niche, and build a career that works for you.

Let's get to it.

Chapter 8

Long-Term Career Growth in Cybersecurity

You've built your foundation. You're working in the field. You've grown your skills, expanded your network, and started making a name for yourself. Now it's time to ask a new question: *Where do I want to go from here?*

This is the chapter where you stop thinking like a beginner and start thinking like a strategist.

Cybersecurity isn't a single lane—it's an entire ecosystem. There are technical tracks, governance paths, leadership roles, hybrid positions, niche specialties, and room to pivot whenever your interests evolve. Whether you want to become a deep-dive technical expert, lead a blue team, architect secure systems, or manage compliance for a Fortune 500 company, there's space for you here.

In this chapter, we'll explore how to choose a specialty that fits your strengths, what it really means to move into mid- and senior-level roles, and how to lead with or without a title. We'll also cover advanced certifications, alternate career paths, and how to think about your future in 2-, 5-, or 10-year blocks.

Because once you've broken into cybersecurity, the next big challenge is building a career that's not just successful—but meaningful.

Let's map it out.

Don't Stop at "Entry-Level"

Getting into cybersecurity is a huge accomplishment—but it's not the end game. It's the beginning.

So many people treat their first role like a final destination. They study hard, grind through labs and certs, land that job—and then... stall. Not because they've stopped caring, but because they don't know what comes next. They made it past the gate, but no one gave them a map for what's beyond it.

Entry-level is just the foundation. You've proven that you can learn the tools, do the work, and contribute to a team. Now it's time to start thinking about how you want to grow—on purpose. The good news? Cybersecurity is one of the few fields where you can pivot and climb at the same time. You're not locked into one role, one track, or one type of work.

You might go deep into detection and response. You might discover a passion for policy and compliance. You might move toward cloud architecture, malware analysis, or even security product management. You might shift between red and blue teams. You can experiment. You can evolve. You can build a path that fits *you*—not someone else's idea of success.

The important thing is to realize that your learning doesn't stop when you get hired. In many ways, that's when the real growth begins.

So, if you're asking, "What's next?"—you're asking the right question.

Choosing Your Specialty or Focus Area

Cybersecurity isn't one job, it's a universe of roles, disciplines, and specialties. Once you've got your foundation in place, it's time to zoom in on the areas that genuinely interest you. This is where your career starts to take shape—not based on where you started, but on where you want to grow.

Don't stress if you're not 100% sure what your "thing" is yet. Your first few years are the perfect time to explore, test, and pivot. You'll naturally gravitate toward certain types of work, tools, or challenges. Pay attention to that. Are you fascinated by uncovering patterns in logs? Maybe threat hunting is for you. Do you love scripting and automation? Security engineering or DevSecOps might be your path. Prefer policies, frameworks, and risk analysis? GRC could be your genius zone.

Let's break down a few of the most common focus areas.

Technical Deep Dives

These are the roles where you stay close to the tech, the tools, and the hands-on work:

- **Threat Hunting:** Proactively searching for threats that evade detection tools. Requires deep knowledge of environments, attacker behavior, and log analysis.

- **Malware Analysis:** Reverse engineering malware samples to understand behavior, tactics, and defense mechanisms.

- **Red Teaming / Offensive Security:** Simulating real-world attacks to test defenses. Involves ethical hacking, social engineering, and exploitation.

- **Security Engineering:** Designing and implementing secure systems. Think firewalls, IAM systems, endpoint protection, SIEMs, and architecture.

- **Cloud Security:** Securing infrastructure in AWS, Azure, or GCP. Focuses on IAM, misconfigurations, policy enforcement, and cloud-native threats.

- **DFIR (Digital Forensics & Incident Response):** Investigating incidents, tracing intrusions, and helping orgs recover while preserving evidence.

Strategic & Governance Roles

These roles lean more into planning, policy, compliance, and risk—but they're still deeply impactful:

- **GRC Lead / Risk Manager:** Ensures the organizations are meeting regulatory, legal, and risk obligations. Requires understanding of frameworks and business alignment.

- **Security Program Manager:** Oversees teams, projects, and security initiatives across departments.

- **Privacy Officer:** Handles data privacy compliance, user rights, and secure data handling.

- **Compliance Auditor:** Reviews systems and practices for alignment with standards like ISO 27001, NIST 800-53, SOC 2, and others.

Hybrid Roles

These blend the technical with the strategic—and often bridge gaps between teams:

- **DevSecOps Engineer:** Builds security into development pipelines. You'll work with developers and operations teams to embed testing, scanning, and secure configurations from code to deployment.

- **Cybersecurity Architect:** Designs secure systems from the ground up. This role requires both technical depth and big-picture thinking.

- **Security Product Manager:** Works on the business and user side of security tools—managing roadmaps, solving user problems, and guiding development.

- **Threat Intelligence Analyst:** Gathers and interprets data about threats, actors, and campaigns to proactively strengthen defenses.

Each of these areas has its own tools, mindsets, and career paths. Some are deeply technical. Others are policy-driven, people-focused, or strategy-heavy. There's no "better" path—only the one that fits your strengths and goals.

This is your invitation to explore. Try a side project in cloud. Shadow a GRC analyst. Take on a red team challenge. See what lights you up. Because once you find your lane, things start moving faster—and the opportunities become way more exciting.

Climbing to Mid-Level and Senior Roles

If entry-level is about proving you can do the work, mid-level and senior roles are about showing you can do it with *depth*, *consistency*, and *impact*. This is where your value shifts from just executing tasks to owning outcomes—and helping others succeed along the way.

So, what makes someone "senior" in cybersecurity?

Other than a promotion and title change, it usually takes a few years on the job. It's about how you think, how you communicate, and how you show up. Senior professionals are the ones who take the initiative, solve problems without handholding, and can explain complex issues clearly to both technical and non-technical audiences. They're the people others turn to when things go sideways—not just for answers, but for calm, strategic direction.

To move into these roles, you need to start thinking beyond the task list. Don't just resolve an alert—understand why it happened, what it could've led to, and how to prevent it in the future. Don't just write documentation, write it so clearly that someone else could follow it in a high-stress incident. Don't just patch a system—know the risk it addressed, the policy it affected, and the compliance implication.

You also want to start mentoring others, even informally. If a junior analyst joins the team, offer to walk them through the ticketing system or explain how you handle false positives. If someone's struggling with scripting, share a tool you built or offer to pair up on a project. Being the person who lifts others up is one of the strongest signals of senior-level maturity.

Here are a few titles to keep your eye on as you grow:

- **Senior Security Analyst** – More autonomy, deeper analysis, often responsible for mentoring junior staff and improving workflows.

- **Security Engineer II** – Mid-level role focused on implementing and maintaining security tools and infrastructure.

- **Red Team Operator / Pen Test Lead** – Conducts and leads offensive security assessments, often with reporting responsibilities.

- **Security Architect** – Designs secure systems and infrastructure, often bridging IT, engineering, and business.

- **GRC Manager / Compliance Lead** – Oversees risk management and policy, aligning security with business objectives.

These aren't just job upgrades, they're mindset upgrades. They require emotional intelligence, adaptability, technical sharpness, and a bigger-picture view of how cybersecurity fits into the business.

The path to senior isn't about checking boxes, it's about growing into someone others trust with the hard stuff.

Going Beyond the Tools

At the start of your cybersecurity journey, it's all about tools. Learning Wireshark, setting up Splunk, running Nmap scans, cracking a TryHackMe room—that's how you build your foundation. And those tools are important. But if you want to grow into a true professional, you eventually have to go beyond the tools.

Why? Because tools change. Vendors change. Technologies evolve. What stays consistent is how you think, how you approach risk, how you design systems, how you respond when things break.

At the next level, it's not enough to know how to *use* the tool. You need to understand why it's being used. What problem is it solving? How does it fit into the broader architecture? What would happen if it failed? That's the kind of thinking that separates mid-level analysts from security leaders.

Start shifting your mindset toward strategy. If you're on a blue team, learn to think like an attacker to have better ideas on how to best defend. If you're in GRC, learn to speak the language of risk in a way that resonates with executives. If you're in engineering, learn how to build defensible systems from the ground up—not just patch problems after the fact.

There are a few areas worth digging into, no matter your role:

- **Risk-based decision making** – Learn how to assess the likelihood and impact of threats. This helps you prioritize what matters and justify your decisions.

- **Incident response strategy** – Go beyond "what button do I push?" and ask, "What's our process? Who needs to be informed? What's our communication plan?"

- **Compliance frameworks** – Understand how standards like NIST, ISO 27001, or SOC 2 shape policies and practices—even if you're not in GRC.

- **Secure design principles** – Especially if you're touching cloud or dev environments. Learn about least privilege, secure defaults, zero trust, and how to bake security into the architecture before problems appear.

These are the kinds of skills that make you valuable far beyond your keyboard. They position you as someone who understands both the technology and the mission—and that's what every team needs more of.

Tools will always be part of the job. But your ability to think critically, connect dots, and make smart decisions? That's what turns you into a trusted expert.

Pursuing Advanced Certifications

By now, you know that certifications aren't golden tickets—but they *can* be powerful tools when used with purpose. At the start of your career, you probably picked up entry-level certs to open doors and build foundational knowledge. As you grow, it's time to be more strategic. The question isn't "Which cert should I chase next?"—it's "What do I need to learn, and which cert aligns with that?"

Advanced certifications aren't about proving you're smart, they're about proving you can solve specific kinds of problems. They show depth in a focus area, signal that you're ready for more responsibility, and in many cases, help justify promotions or salary bumps. But they're also expensive and time-consuming, so make sure you're choosing certs that match your actual goals, not just what's trending on LinkedIn.

Here's a quick look at popular options based on your career track:

Technical / Red Team:

- *OSCP (Offensive Security Certified Professional):* Known for its hands-on 24-hour exam. It's a serious test of persistence and practical skill—great for aspiring penetration testers or red teamers.

- *OSWE (Web Exploitation):* A more advanced cert focused on web application security and exploitation.

- *CRTO (Certified Red Team Operator):* Focuses on advanced adversary emulation and Active Directory attacks.

Blue Team / SOC / Incident Response:

- *GCIA (Intrusion Analyst):* Deep dive into packet analysis, IDS/IPS tuning, and network-level detection.

- *GCIH (Incident Handler):* Covers incident response tactics, malware handling, and attack detection.

- *GCFA (Forensics Analyst):* Heavy focus on digital forensics, disk and memory analysis—ideal for DFIR roles.

- *Splunk Power User:* Vendor cert, but highly respected for SIEM work and log analysis.

Cloud Security:

- *AWS Security Specialty:* A top-tier cert for cloud security professionals working in Amazon Web Services environments.

- *Azure SC-300:* Covers identity and access, security operations, and compliance in Microsoft Azure.

- *CCSP (Certified Cloud Security Professional):* Broad cloud security certification from ISC2—great for architects, engineers, and GRC pros alike.

GRC / Management:

- *CISA (Certified Information Systems Auditor):* Strong for auditors, risk managers, and compliance roles.

- *CRISC (Certified in Risk and Information Systems Control):* Focuses on enterprise risk and controls—valuable in leadership and governance roles.

- *CISSP (Certified Information Systems Security Professional):* One of the most well-known certs in cybersecurity leadership. Covers eight domains and requires real-world experience to be fully certified.

Remember, certs are tools—not titles. They don't replace experience, but they can sharpen your skills, validate your knowledge, and get your résumé past HR filters when paired with hands-on work.

If your company offers training budgets or certification reimbursement, don't be shy—ask. Many organizations are happy to invest in motivated team members, especially if the knowledge gained helps improve team capability.

One final note: you don't need to rush. Take on certifications when they make sense, not just to fill space on your LinkedIn. A well-timed, well-earned certification can do a lot—but it's your skills, attitude, and initiative that will carry you the furthest.

Becoming a Leader Without a Title

Leadership isn't about your job title, it's about how you show up. You don't need to be a manager, director, or team lead to make a real impact. In fact, some of the best leaders in cybersecurity are the people who step up before they're ever asked to.

So, what does that look like?

It means mentoring the new hire who's still learning the ropes, even if you're just a few months ahead of them. It means writing clear documentation, so the next person doesn't have to guess what you figured out. It means spotting a broken process, improving it, and sharing the solution with your team—because it makes everyone's job easier.

Leadership also looks like taking responsibility when things go wrong. Being the person who stays calm during an incident, focuses on solutions, and helps the team get back on track without finger-pointing. It's knowing when to ask for help, and when to offer it.

You can run a tabletop exercise. You can start a weekly "threat of the week" chat. You can organize lunch-and-learns or help junior staff get through their first alert review. These things might not show up in your job description, but they show up where it matters: in how people see you, trust you, and rely on you.

When you lead without a title, *people start to see you as someone who should have one*. That's how promotions happen. That's how you earn influence. Not because you demanded it—but because you've already been doing the work.

Leadership is a mindset. It's a habit. And it starts the moment you decide to raise your hand and add value—without waiting for permission.

Should You Go into Management?

At some point in your cybersecurity journey, you might start thinking about management. Maybe someone suggests it. Maybe a leadership role opens up. Or maybe you're just curious if that's the next logical step. It's a good question—but it's not one you want to answer on autopilot.

Let's get something out of the way first: management isn't a promotion, it's a shift. It's not "leveling up" from hands-on work. It's changing lanes entirely.

When you move into management, your time is no longer your own. You're now responsible for people, priorities, meetings, planning, performance reviews, team health, and long-term strategy. You won't be spending most of your time analyzing logs or configuring tools. Instead, you'll be helping your team do their best work—removing blockers, provide feedback, handling conflict, and representing their needs to upper leadership.

That might sound exciting to you—or it might sound like a nightmare. And either reaction is okay. Great cybersecurity teams need strong individual contributors *and* thoughtful managers. One path isn't better than the other. They're just different.

So how do you know if you're ready to step into a management role?

You might be ready if:

- You enjoy mentoring and helping others grow
- You want to shape how your team works, not just what they work on
- You're willing to deal with ambiguity, people problems, and organizational politics
- You find satisfaction in building systems, not just solving technical puzzles

You might want to wait if:

- You still love the technical work and want to go deeper

- You're not ready to give up control of your own hands-on tasks

- You don't feel energized by managing people, meetings, or conflict

If you're on the fence, talk to someone in a management role you respect. Ask what their days look like. What they love about the job. What's hard? What they wish they'd known. Real-world perspective beats guesswork every time.

And remember you can always explore management and step back if it's not the right fit. Some of the best tech leads, architects, and principal engineers tried management, learned from it, and returned to individual contributor roles stronger than ever.

Management isn't a destination. It's a path—just like any other. Choose it because it fits your strengths and your goals, not because you think it's what you're "supposed" to do next.

Alternate Career Paths Within Cyber

Not everyone wants to follow the traditional route. And in cybersecurity, that's more than okay, it's normal. This field has a wide-open door for people who think differently, build differently, or just want more control over how and where they work.

Let's look at a few alternate paths that might align with your personality, lifestyle, or long-term goals:

Freelancing or Consulting

Want more freedom over your time, your clients, and your income? Freelancing might be your lane. As a freelance or independent consultant, you can offer services like security assessments, vulnerability testing, policy writing, or training workshops. Many small businesses and startups need help but can't afford full-time staff. That's where you come in. It takes hustle to build a client base, but it's doable—and it pays well once you're established.

Security Startups

Working at a startup isn't for everyone, but if you like fast-paced environments and wearing multiple hats, it can be incredibly rewarding. You'll often get to shape products, build processes from scratch, and learn at a speed you won't find in a larger company. Just know that startups can be chaotic—so flexibility, grit, and curiosity are key.

Government and DoD Roles

Cybersecurity in the public sector is a whole world of its own. Whether you're working for a city, state, or federal agency—or pursuing contract work through DoD channels, these roles are mission-driven and often come with job security, strong benefits, and meaningful work protecting national infrastructure or public data. If you already have a clearance, or are open to getting one, this path opens even more doors.

Academic and Research Careers

Love to investigate, write, or study deep technical topics? Academic roles, cyber research institutions, and think tanks are always looking for people who can analyze trends, dig into threat actor behavior, or publish insights on malware, vulnerabilities, or security economics. This is especially fulfilling for those who like working on the frontier of what's next in cybersecurity.

Education, Training, and Advocacy

As you grow, you might discover you love teaching others—through bootcamps, workshops, awareness training, or even full-time instruction. Some pros transition into curriculum design, content development, or cybersecurity advocacy work. It's a great way to influence the next generation while staying connected to the field.

There's more than one way to build a meaningful career in cybersecurity. You don't have to chase titles or follow someone else's path. You get to define what success looks like for you—based on your values, your strengths, and the kind of impact you want to make.

Whether you're dreaming about running your own consultancy, building a security tool, teaching in a classroom, or defending federal infrastructure, know this: the field is wide open.

If the unconventional path is for you, go for it. You just need a plan—and the willingness to walk it.

Planning the Next 5 Years

You don't need a 20-year plan. But you *do* need a rough idea of where you're heading.

In cybersecurity, things move fast. New roles pop up, technologies evolve, and the skills that are hot today might shift tomorrow. That's why it helps to zoom out every so often and ask yourself: *Where am I trying to go? What kind of work do I want to be doing? What kind of professional do I want to become?*

Start by thinking in 1–2 year blocks. What's the next big step you want to take? Maybe it's moving into a new specialization, getting hands-on with cloud, taking on more responsibility in your current role, or finally earning that cert you've been eyeing. Then zoom out to a 5-year vision. Where do you want to land? Senior red teamer? Cloud architect? GRC lead? Maybe even your own consultancy?

To get there, set clear and realistic milestones. For example:

- Year 1–2: Deepen your specialty, earn an advanced cert, lead a project, mentor a new teammate.

- Year 3–4: Transition into a senior role, speak at a local event, contribute to open-source or community tools.

- Year 5: Target a leadership position, shift into a niche role, or launch something on your own—like a podcast, product, or training program.

Along the way, reevaluate. Your goals *will* change. What you're passionate about now might evolve. That's normal. Check in with yourself annually. What do you enjoy most about your current role? What drains you? What skills are you building without even realizing it? Use that intel to adjust your course.

Also, don't forget to celebrate the wins. Passing a hard exam. Getting a shoutout from your manager. Helping a teammate through an incident. These moments are more than career milestones—they're proof that you're growing, adapting, and making an impact.

Your cybersecurity journey isn't a straight line—it's a series of choices, experiments, and pivots. But if you stay curious, stay intentional, and keep showing up, you'll end up exactly where you're meant to be.

Chapter 9

Your Cybersecurity Journey Has Just Begun

If you've made it this far, pause and take a breath—because you've done more than you think. You picked up this book, stayed with it, and showed up for yourself. That's not a small thing.

You might've started with doubts—wondering if this field was possible for someone like you. Maybe you didn't know where to begin, or if you even belonged. But now, you understand the roles, the tools, the certs, and the skills. You've built labs, made connections, solved problems, and taken action. You're no longer just curious. You're capable.

Cybersecurity no longer feels out of reach. It feels real. Tangible. Yours. And the journey? It's just getting started.

Own Your Progress—And Your Path

It's easy to miss how far you've come when your head's down, focused on learning. But pause for a second. When you started, cybersecurity might've felt confusing or out of reach. Now, concepts like threat hunting or cloud security feel like possibilities—not mysteries.

Wherever you came from—military, IT, education, hospitality, or completely outside tech—it doesn't matter. What matters is what you're doing with it. Your background isn't a gap to close; it's a strength. It helps you see things others might miss.

There's no single right way into cybersecurity. Don't waste time comparing your timeline to someone else's. Own your story. Own your progress. You belong here, and your voice matters.

How to Keep Moving Forward

Cybersecurity isn't something you learn once and move on from. It evolves daily. To stay in it—and thrive—you need three things: curiosity, consistency, and humility.

Stay curious. Keep asking questions. Dig into how things work and why they break. Let your interests guide you.

Stay consistent. You don't need ten-hour study days. You need steady effort. A few labs, a weekly post, regular reflection—it all adds up.

Stay humble. No one knows it all. Be honest about what you don't know. Be willing to try, to fail, and to get better.

Here's how to stay grounded:

- Check in with yourself every 3–6 months. What's changed? What excites you now?

- Stay active in the community. Join a Discord server. Leave a comment. Ask a question.

- Track your wins. Write them down. Look back when you hit doubt.

- Teach someone else what you just learned. It reinforces everything.

- Ask this often: *What can I learn today?*

Small steps done often are what move careers forward. Just keep going.

You Are Now Part of a Bigger Mission

Cybersecurity isn't just about tech—it's about trust, safety, and stability. Behind every alert, policy, or script is a person, a system, or a business you're protecting.

You might defend a small business. You might stop a phishing attack. You might help someone understand how to stay safe online. Whatever your role, the impact is real.

This work matters. You matter. You're part of something bigger now. Never lose sight of the mission behind the work.

You Made It

Thank you for sticking with this journey. If you've read this far, you've already proven you're serious. That you care. That you're willing to do the work.

You don't need to be a genius or a hacker to succeed. You need heart, hustle, and hunger to keep learning. The best people in this field are the ones who stay curious, help others, and never stop improving.

Cybersecurity isn't just a job. It's a calling. And now that you've heard it—it's time to answer.

Your journey is just beginning. Go build something great.

ALL THE WAY! AIRBORNE!

Glossary

Authentication: The process of verifying that a user or system is who they claim to be. In practice, this might involve checking a password, fingerprint, or another form of identification before granting access.

Authorization: The process of determining what an authenticated user or system is allowed to do. It defines the permissions or access levels someone has—deciding, for example, which files they can read or which actions they can perform after they've logged in.

Blue Team: The defenders in cybersecurity who focus on protecting an organization's systems and data. Blue team members monitor for attacks, strengthen defenses (like setting up firewalls and security policies), and respond to incidents to keep attackers out.

CIA Triad (Confidentiality, Integrity, Availability): The three fundamental principles of cybersecurity. Confidentiality means keeping information secret from unauthorized people, Integrity means ensuring information is accurate and unaltered, and Availability means making sure information and systems are accessible when needed.

CEH (Certified Ethical Hacker): A professional certification for ethical hacking. It teaches security practitioners how to think and act like a hacker (legally and with permission) to find weaknesses in systems, so those weaknesses can be fixed before bad actors exploit them.

CISA (Certified Information Systems Auditor): A certification focused on auditing and assessing an organization's IT and security systems. Professionals with a CISA understand how to review processes and controls, ensuring that companies follow best practices and comply with laws or standards in cybersecurity and IT governance.

CISM (Certified Information Security Manager): A certification aimed at management-level security professionals. It demonstrates knowledge of developing and managing an organization's information security program—covering governance, risk management, compliance, and incident handling from a leadership perspective.

CISO (Chief Information Security Officer): A senior executive responsible for an organization's cybersecurity strategy and programs. The CISO oversees the security team, sets security policies, manages risk at the highest level, and ensures that the company's information and systems are well-**protected against threats.**

CISSP (Certified Information Systems Security Professional): A widely respected advanced cybersecurity certification. CISSP covers a broad range of security topics (from network security and software development security to risk management) and is often required or preferred for senior security roles; it typically requires substantial experience in the field.

Cloud Security: Protecting data, applications, and services that run in cloud environments (such as Amazon Web Services, Microsoft Azure, or Google Cloud). Cloud security involves ensuring that cloud setups are configured safely, controlling who can access cloud resources, and keeping data stored in the cloud safe from unauthorized access or leaks.

CompTIA Security+: An entry-level certification that covers the fundamentals of cybersecurity. Security+ ensures the holder understands basic topics like networks, threats and attacks (for example, malware and phishing), cryptography (encryption), and security best practices; it's often recommended as a first cybersecurity certification for beginners and is recognized by many employers.

Data Breach: A security incident where sensitive or confidential information is accessed, stolen, or exposed by an unauthorized person. In a data breach, things like personal data, financial records, or passwords might be leaked—often leading to loss of privacy, financial harm, or reputational damage to the organization that was breached.

DDoS (Distributed Denial of Service): A type of attack that attempts to make a computer or network service (like a website) unavailable by overwhelming it with a flood of internet traffic. In a DDoS attack, an attacker uses many computers (often infected machines called a botnet) to send an enormous number of requests to the target, causing it to slow down or crash, so legitimate users can't access it.

DevSecOps (Development, Security, and Operations): An approach to software development that integrates security at every phase of the DevOps process. In DevSecOps, developers, security specialists, and IT operations work together from the start—meaning security checks and fixes are built into the pipeline of coding, testing, and releasing software, rather than being added at the end.

Digital Forensics: The practice of investigating digital devices and media to uncover evidence of cyber incidents or crimes. Digital forensics experts retrieve and analyze data from computers, smartphones, networks, etc., to figure out what happened during a security breach (for example, determining how an attacker got in or what data was taken), all while preserving that information for possible legal use.

Encryption: A method of protecting information by transforming it into a secret code so that it looks like gibberish to anyone who doesn't have the key to decode it. When data is encrypted (whether it's a file, message, or connection), only someone with the correct decryption key or password can convert it back into its readable form, keeping the information confidential from eavesdroppers.

Endpoint Security: Security measures aimed at individual devices (endpoints) like laptops, desktops, tablets, and smartphones. It typically involves using software tools such as antivirus programs, anti-malware scanners, and endpoint detection and response (EDR) systems to prevent, detect, and remove threats on those devices, since each device can be a target for attackers.

Firewall: A network security tool (it can be hardware, software, or both) that acts as a gatekeeper for incoming and outgoing network traffic. A firewall follows a set of rules to decide which traffic is safe to allow through and which to block, helping to prevent unauthorized access to a network, much like a security guard that lets trusted visitors in but keeps suspicious traffic out.

GRC (Governance, Risk, and Compliance): A management approach in cybersecurity that deals with high-level security policies and regulations. Governance is about setting rules and strategies for security, Risk management is about identifying and handling potential security problems before they occur, and Compliance is about following laws, regulations, and standards (like HIPAA or PCI-DSS) that apply to cybersecurity. In simpler terms, GRC ensures a company is doing the right things to stay secure and meet requirements.

GRC Analyst: A cybersecurity professional who specializes in Governance, Risk, and Compliance. A GRC analyst helps an organization create and enforce security policies, assess and prioritize risks (like figuring out what could go wrong and how to prevent it), ensure compliance with legal and industry security standards, and prepare for audits. This role is more about paperwork, planning, and strategy than hands-on hacking—focusing on the "rules and procedures" side of cybersecurity.

IAM (Identity and Access Management): Practices and tools for managing who is allowed to do what within an IT environment. IAM is about making sure the right people (or computer systems) have the appropriate access to technology resources: it covers creating user accounts, setting passwords, adding or removing access rights, and using technologies like single sign-on or two-factor authentication to control and verify user identities.

IDS/IPS (Intrusion Detection/Prevention System): Security systems that watch network or computer activities for malicious behavior. An IDS (Intrusion Detection System) monitors and alerts if it sees something suspicious or known to be a threat, like a burglar alarm for your network. An IPS (Intrusion Prevention System) goes a step further by automatically blocking or stopping the detected malicious activity, not just warning about it.

Incident Response: The organized approach and procedures an organization uses to address and manage a cybersecurity incident (like a data breach or malware outbreak). Incident response typically involves steps like detecting the problem, containing and removing the threat, recovering affected systems or data, and then analyzing what happened to learn lessons and improve future security measures.

IoT (Internet of Things): A term for everyday devices and objects that connect to the internet and can send or receive data. Examples include smart thermostats, fitness wearables, internet-connected cameras, or even smart appliances. In cybersecurity, IoT is important because these devices need to be secured—if a smart fridge or a Wi-Fi light bulb isn't properly protected, it could be exploited by hackers as an entry point into a network or to steal information.

Kali Linux: A specialized version of the Linux operating system that's packed with cybersecurity tools, used mainly by ethical hackers and penetration testers. Kali Linux comes pre-loaded with programs for scanning networks, testing for vulnerabilities, cracking passwords, and more—essentially providing a one-stop platform for learning about and performing cybersecurity tasks.

Least Privilege: A core security principle that says any user or system should have only the minimum access rights or permissions necessary to do their job. By giving everyone the least amount of privilege needed, the damage from accidents or attacks is limited—if an account is compromised or a mistake is made, the intruder or error doesn't have free rein over everything, just the smaller set of resources that account really needed to use.

Malware: Short for "malicious software," this term describes any software designed to harm, exploit, or illegally access a computer system. Malware comes in many forms, including viruses, worms, trojan horses, spyware, and ransomware—and can do things like steal data, spy on user activities, damage files, or give attackers control over a device. Defending against malware is a big part of what cybersecurity is all about.

MFA (Multi-Factor Authentication): A security process that requires a user to provide two or more verification factors to prove they are who they claim to be, before gaining access to an account or system. Instead of just entering a password (one factor), a user might also have to enter a code from their smartphone or provide a fingerprint. The idea is that even if one factor (like a password) is compromised, an attacker still can't get in without the other factor(s), dramatically increasing account security.

Nmap: A free, open-source tool used for network scanning and reconnaissance. Security professionals and system admins use Nmap to discover devices on a network, find open ports (doors for communication), and identify what services or software those devices are running. In short, Nmap helps map out the network and can highlight potential entry points or vulnerabilities that need securing.

OSINT (Open Source Intelligence): The practice of gathering information from publicly available sources, especially during investigations or security assessments. In cybersecurity, OSINT might include searching websites, social media, forums, and public records to collect data about a person or organization. This information could be used by defenders to understand what an attacker might easily find out about their target, or by attackers to plan a targeted approach—so managing your public information footprint is part of security too.

OSCP (Offensive Security Certified Professional): A well-known advanced certification for ethical hackers and penetration testers. The OSCP is respected because to earn it, candidates must pass a hands-on exam where they try to break into a series of test systems in a lab within a time limit. It proves that the holder has practical, real-world hacking skills—showing they can not only find vulnerabilities but also exploit them and document what they did, all under pressure.

OWASP Top 10: A list of the ten most critical web application security risks, published by the Open Web Application Security Project (OWASP). It highlights common vulnerabilities that web developers and security pros should be aware of—such as SQL injection (inserting malicious code into databases), cross-site scripting (injecting malicious scripts into web pages), and other frequent web application weaknesses. The OWASP Top 10 is essentially a checklist of "what not to do" when building or testing web apps, helping teams prioritize fixing these major issues.

Patch Management: The routine process of updating software and systems with patches, which are small pieces of code that fix bugs or security vulnerabilities. Good patch management means regularly applying these updates (for example, updating your operating system or applications when a security fix is released) so that known weaknesses are corrected—this reduces the chances that attackers can exploit a known flaw to break in or cause harm.

Penetration Testing: An authorized, simulated cyberattack on a computer system, network, or application, performed to evaluate the security of the system. Often shortened to "pen testing," it's basically ethical hacking: professionals (penetration testers) use the same tools and techniques as attackers would, trying to find and exploit vulnerabilities. The end goal is to identify security weaknesses so they can be fixed before real attackers find them.

Phishing: A common type of online scam or attack where attackers impersonate a legitimate entity or trusted person to trick someone into revealing sensitive information or installing malware. Phishing often happens through fake emails or messages—for example, an email that looks like it's from a bank or a colleague might urge you to click a link or open an attachment. If you fall for it, you might end up giving away your passwords, credit card numbers, or infecting your device with malicious software.

Ransomware: A form of malware that locks you out of your computer or encrypts your files, essentially holding your data hostage. The attackers then demand a ransom payment (often in cryptocurrency) in exchange for giving you back access to your data. For example, you might turn on your computer to find all your files encrypted and a note saying you must pay $300 in Bitcoin to get a decryption key. Ransomware attacks can cause huge disruptions and losses, and there's no guarantee that paying the ransom will actually restore the data.

Red Team: The offensive side of a cybersecurity exercise, often a group of ethical hackers who simulate real-world attack techniques to test an organization's defenses. A red team's job is to think like an adversary and try to breach security—finding ways into networks, applications, or facilities (with permission from the organization). Their findings (how they got in, what they could access) are then used to strengthen the defense. In short, the red team exposes weaknesses so the blue team (defenders) can fix them.

Risk: The potential for loss or damage when something valuable is threatened. In cybersecurity, risk is usually thought of as the combination of a threat and a vulnerability: it's the chance that a threat (like a hacker or malware) will exploit a vulnerability (like an unpatched software flaw) and cause harm, plus an idea of how bad that harm could be. Organizations assess risk to decide where to focus their security efforts—tackling the biggest risks first by reducing vulnerabilities and preparing for threats.

SIEM (Security Information and Event Management): A technology platform or tool that aggregates (collects) and analyzes activity from many different sources across a network (such as logs from servers, applications, firewalls, and other security devices). A SIEM helps make sense of this mountain of data by correlating events and flagging unusual or suspicious patterns in real time. In practice, it might alert the security team if it notices, say, a user account trying to log in to hundreds of machines (which could indicate a spreading attack) or if a normally quiet server suddenly floods the network with data. Essentially, a SIEM is a centralized alarm system and detective for cybersecurity, helping teams spot and respond to possible incidents quickly.

Security Operations Center (SOC): A team or dedicated facility where an organization's cybersecurity is monitored and managed. The SOC is like a command center for defense: SOC analysts work in shifts to watch over the company's networks and systems 24/7, using dashboards and alerts (often from tools like SIEMs) to detect potential threats. When something suspicious happens, the SOC coordinates the investigation and response. In summary, a Security Operations Center is the front line hub where defenders keep an eye on everything and react to keep the organization safe.

SOC Analyst: A member of the Security Operations Center team, typically responsible for monitoring security tools and responding to alerts. A SOC analyst's day-to-day work might include reviewing logs and notifications for signs of malware or intrusions, investigating anything unusual (like a strange login or a flagged email), and following runbooks or procedures to handle minor incidents or escalate serious ones. This role is often entry-level in cybersecurity and is crucial as the "eyes on glass" that can catch threats early and help stop security incidents in their tracks.

Social Engineering: A technique attackers use that focuses on tricking or manipulating people, rather than hacking computer systems, to gain unauthorized access or information. Social engineering plays on human psychology—common examples include someone pretending to be tech support to get a password reset, an urgent phone call asking for financial info, or an email that tugs at emotions (like fear or curiosity) to get the victim to click a malicious link. Since humans can be the weakest link in security, social engineering is a major concern and is addressed through training and awareness.

Threat: Anything that can potentially cause harm to a system, network, or organization. In cybersecurity, a threat could be a malicious attacker (like a hacker or insider), a piece of malware, or even an event like a hardware failure or natural disaster. It's basically the "danger" in the security equation— the actor or event that might exploit a weakness and lead to a negative outcome.

Threat Hunting: A proactive security practice where experts actively search through systems and networks to find signs of hidden threats or attackers that haven't been detected by automated tools. Instead of just waiting for alarms to go off, threat hunters use their knowledge of attacker behavior and system vulnerabilities to look for clues or anomalies (for example, odd patterns in network traffic or unusual account activity) that could indicate an undetected attack in progress. The goal is to catch sneaky threats early, before they cause significant damage.

VPN (Virtual Private Network): A service or technology that creates an encrypted "tunnel" through the internet, allowing you to connect securely to another network as if you were on a private network. People often use VPNs to protect their data on public Wi-Fi (the encryption prevents others from snooping on your traffic) or to remotely access a workplace network securely from home. In simple terms, a VPN keeps your online connection private and secure by scrambling the data you send and receive and routing it through a trusted server.

Vulnerability: A weakness or flaw in a system that could be exploited by an attacker to cause harm or gain unauthorized access. Vulnerabilities can be caused by software bugs, outdated programs, poor configuration, or even human factors (like weak passwords). For example, if a website has a coding mistake that lets someone sneak in and bypass the login, that mistake is a vulnerability. Identifying and fixing vulnerabilities (through patches, updates, or configuration changes) is critical to reducing risk.

Vulnerability Assessment: A systematic process of scanning and evaluating systems to find known weaknesses and security flaws. During a vulnerability assessment, automated tools (and sometimes manual techniques) are used to identify vulnerabilities like missing patches or misconfigured settings. The result is usually a report that prioritizes the vulnerabilities found, so an organization knows which issues to fix first to strengthen their security. It's a key preventive measure, like a regular health check-up for computers and networks to catch problems before attackers do.

Wireshark: A popular free tool for analyzing network traffic in detail. Using Wireshark, a security professional or network admin can capture data packets traveling over a network (like the contents of network messages, not including encrypted ones) and then inspect them. It's like using a microscope on your network's data: Wireshark can show, for instance, what information is being sent from your computer to a website or help troubleshoot network issues. In cybersecurity, it's useful for diagnosing problems, analyzing suspicious network activity, or understanding exactly what kind of data is moving through your environment.

Zero-day: A security vulnerability that is unknown to the software or hardware vendor and thus has no official fix or patch yet. Because the vendor literally has "zero days" of warning to address it, attackers can exploit a zero-day vulnerability before it's patched, making it particularly dangerous. When hackers use a zero-day (for example, a hidden flaw in a web browser that even its makers aren't aware of), they can often succeed since no one has had the chance to close that security hole.

Zero Trust: A security model that assumes no user or device—whether inside or outside the organization's network—is automatically trustworthy. In a zero trust approach, verification is required every time someone tries to access a resource: this means continually checking identities, permissions, and the security posture of devices. The philosophy is "never trust, always verify," which helps contain breaches; even if an attacker gets into the network, they still have to keep authenticating to move around, which makes it harder for them to do damage.

Resources and References

Below is a compilation of notable resources and references mentioned throughout *The Cybersecurity Field Guide*. They are organized by category for clarity. Each item includes a brief description and a hyperlink to an official or authoritative source.

Online Platforms and Labs

Coursera – A major online learning platform hosting courses and professional certificate programs (including the Google Cybersecurity Professional Certificate) from top universities and companies. Many courses can be audited for free, with optional paid certificates for completion. *(Official site: coursera.org)*

CyberDefenders – An online CTF platform focused on blue team (defensive) challenges and digital forensics exercises. It provides realistic incident response and threat-hunting scenarios for those interested in analysis and defense. *(Official site: cyberdefenders.org)*

Cybrary – A cybersecurity education platform offering a mix of free and premium courses on security fundamentals, cloud, SOC analysis, and more. It features guided career paths for roles like SOC Analyst or Cloud Security to help learners structure their training. *(Official site: cybrary.io)*

edX – A large MOOC provider hosting free online courses from leading institutions (MIT, Harvard, etc.) across various disciplines. edX offers many computer science and cybersecurity courses; like Coursera, content can be accessed for free, and a paid certificate is optional for those who complete the material. *(Official site: edx.org)*

Hack The Box – An online platform featuring virtual machines and labs that simulate real-world security vulnerabilities. Users can practice penetration testing against these challenges. Known for its advanced hacking scenarios, Hack The Box also offers a guided "Starting Point" tier for beginners to learn the basics in a structured way. *(Official site: hackthebox.com)*

Immersive Labs – A fully interactive, on-demand, and gamified cyber skills platform offering challenge-based labs and cyber range exercises. Immersive Labs provides browser-based simulations of real-world cyber scenarios to help individuals and teams build and prove their security capabilities. *(Official site: immersivelabs.com)*

OverTheWire – A community-driven platform that hosts wargames – gamified challenges designed to teach security concepts and Linux fundamentals through the command line. The classic "Bandit" game, for example, guides absolute beginners through basic Linux/CLI skills. OverTheWire's puzzles are fun and educational, helping players practice topics like cryptography, web exploitation, and more. *(Official site: overthewire.org)*

picoCTF – A free, beginner-friendly cybersecurity competition and learning platform created by security experts at Carnegie Mellon University. picoCTF offers challenge-based "capture the flag" exercises that teach participants to find misconfigurations, test passwords, analyze web apps, and more in a fun, hands-on format.

(Official site: picoctf.org)

RangeForce – A browser-based cyber range platform featuring hands-on labs and simulations. The RangeForce Community Edition provides modules on topics such as phishing defense, endpoint security, SIEM log analysis, and other real-world scenarios. It's an interactive way to build skills by tackling challenges defenders face in practice. *(Official site: rangeforce.com)*

TryHackMe – A free online platform for learning cybersecurity through hands-on exercises and labs in the browser. TryHackMe offers guided learning paths, gamified challenges, and an active community, making it one of the best starting points for aspiring cyber professionals. Beginners can start with basic networking or web security rooms and advance to more complex challenges. *(Official site: tryhackme.com)*

Udemy – A global online marketplace for video courses on a wide array of topics. Udemy hosts many affordable courses in IT and cybersecurity—often discounted to under $20 for top-rated content. Learners can find up-to-date courses on ethical hacking, Security+ prep, cloud security, SOC analysis, and more. *(Official site: udemy.com)*

Certifications

AWS Certified Cloud Practitioner – An entry-level Amazon Web Services certification that validates a foundational, high-level understanding of AWS cloud services and terminology. This credential is often the first step for those starting a cloud career, demonstrating core knowledge of AWS's platform and concepts. *(Official AWS page: aws.amazon.com/certification)*

AWS Certified Security – Specialty – An advanced AWS certification that validates expertise in securing AWS environments. It covers topics like data protection, cloud infrastructure security, incident response, identity and access management, and monitoring on AWS. This is intended for experienced professionals who design and implement secure solutions in the AWS Cloud. *(Official AWS page: aws.amazon.com/certification)*

Azure Fundamentals (AZ-900) – Microsoft's entry-level certification for Azure, which "demonstrate[s] foundational knowledge of cloud concepts, core Azure services, plus Azure management and governance features and tools."

 It requires no prior experience and is a starting point for learning Azure services, security basics, and cloud terminology. *(Official Microsoft page: learn.microsoft.com)*

Blue Team Level 1 (BTL1) – A practical junior-level certification (offered by Security Blue Team) designed to train technical defenders in incident response, monitoring, and threat hunting. BTL1 focuses on hands-on blue team skills— candidates learn to defend networks and respond to cyber incidents using tools and techniques actively used by professionals worldwide. *(Official page: securityblue.team)*

Certified Ethical Hacker (CEH) – An intermediate cybersecurity certification from EC-Council that certifies skills in offensive security and penetration testing. As a certified ethical hacker, you use the same techniques as malicious hackers to assess security and identify weaknesses, but for defensive purposes. CEH is often required for DoD roles and covers a broad range of hacking tools and methodologies (footprinting, scanning, exploitation, etc.). *(Official EC-Council page: eccouncil.org)*

Certified Information Security Manager (CISM) – A leading certification from ISACA aimed at professionals in information security management roles. CISM validates expertise in managing and governing an enterprise information security program – focusing on risk management, incident response, and program development. It's highly valued for those pursuing IT security management or CISO-track positions. *(Official ISACA page: isaca.org)*

Certified Information Systems Auditor (CISA) – A globally recognized certification for IS audit, control, and assurance professionals, offered by ISACA. The CISA credential demonstrates expertise in auditing information systems, IT governance and risk management, and protecting information assets. It is widely used as a standard for IT auditors "in audit, control, assurance, and security" roles. *(Official ISACA page: isaca.org)*

Certified Information Systems Security Professional (CISSP) – An elite cybersecurity certification from (ISC)[2] covering eight broad domains of security (including security architecture, operations, asset security, cryptography, etc.).

CISSP is a top-tier, vendor-neutral credential often required for senior security positions, emphasizing security governance, risk management, and architecture design. *(Official (ISC)² page: isc2.org)*

Certified in Cybersecurity (CC) – An entry-level certification from (ISC)² that validates foundational cybersecurity knowledge for those new to the field. (ISC)²'s CC covers the basics across five domains (security principles, business continuity, access controls, network security, and security operations) and "proves you have the foundational knowledge, skills and abilities for an entry- or junior-level cybersecurity role." *(Official (ISC)² page: isc2.org)*

Certified Cloud Security Professional (CCSP) – An advanced certification by (ISC)² for experienced professionals focused on cloud security. CCSP covers best practices in cloud architecture, data security, platform and infrastructure security, application security, and compliance. It is a vendor-neutral credential that demonstrates expertise in securing cloud environments and is often pursued by those with CISSP-level knowledge who specialize in cloud. *(Official (ISC)² page: isc2.org)*

Cisco Certified CyberOps Associate – A certification from Cisco focusing on Security Operations Center (SOC) roles. It validates skills in threat monitoring, detection, and incident response. This cert (formerly Cisco CCNA Cyber Ops) is great for those aiming for blue team analyst positions, covering fundamentals of SOC operations, security monitoring tools, intrusion analysis, and incident handling. *(Official Cisco page: learningnetwork.cisco.com)*

CompTIA A+ – A widely recognized entry-level IT certification that covers foundational knowledge in hardware, networking, operating systems, and basic cybersecurity. CompTIA A+ certifies skills needed for IT support and help desk roles (e.g., troubleshooting PCs, configuring devices, basic network setup). It's often the first cert for those starting an IT career. *(Official CompTIA page: comptia.org)*

CompTIA IT Fundamentals (ITF+) – A beginner certification that introduces absolute newcomers to basic IT concepts. ITF+ covers essential topics like basic computing terminology, infrastructure, software development, and database fundamentals, helping individuals build general tech literacy and confidence. It's not required, but useful for those with non-technical backgrounds exploring IT. *(Official CompTIA page: comptia.org)*

CompTIA PenTest+ – An intermediate-level certification that "focuses on offensive skills through pen testing and vulnerability assessment." PenTest+ validates the ability to plan and scope assessments, exploit networks and applications, perform vulnerability scanning, and report on findings. It's a vendor-neutral alternative for those pursuing penetration testing roles (often seen as between CEH and OSCP in difficulty). *(Official CompTIA page: comptia.org)*

CompTIA Security+ – A globally recognized, vendor-neutral certification that validates foundational cybersecurity knowledge. Security+ covers a broad range of core topics— network security, threats and vulnerabilities, cryptography, risk management, identity and access control, etc. It's often cited as "the gold standard for beginners" in security and is required for many entry-level security jobs (including U.S. DoD

8570 roles). *(Official CompTIA page: comptia.org)*

CompTIA Cybersecurity Analyst (CySA+) – An intermediate cybersecurity certification that focuses on defensive security analytics. CySA+ certifies one's ability to use threat detection tools, interpret data, identify vulnerabilities, and conduct incident response. It's often pursued after Security+; CompTIA describes CySA+ as an analyst certification "with behavioral analytics" skills for monitoring networks and devices. *(Official CompTIA page: comptia.org)*

eLearnSecurity Junior Penetration Tester (eJPT) – An entry-level penetration testing certification from eLearnSecurity/INE. The eJPT exam is a practical, hands-on test where candidates perform actual hacking exercises in a lab environment. Earning eJPT demonstrates a solid grasp of fundamental pentesting skills (network scanning, enumeration, exploitation of basic vulnerabilities) and is a good first cert for aspiring ethical hackers. *(Official INE page: ine.com)*

GIAC Certifications (SANS Institute) – A suite of specialized cybersecurity certifications offered by the SANS Institute's Global Information Assurance Certification program. GIAC certs are highly respected but also costly; each targets a specific skill set. Examples include: GCIH (Certified Incident Handler), GPEN (Penetration Tester), GSEC (Security Essentials), and many others for forensics, defense, and management. GIAC certifications are known for their rigor and real-world focus and are frequently updated to reflect the latest threats. *(Official GIAC site: giac.org)*

Google Cybersecurity Professional Certificate – A beginner-friendly, hands-on training program developed by Google and hosted on Coursera. This certificate program introduces learners to cybersecurity foundations, security tools, and processes through a series of courses and labs. It is designed for those new to the field (especially career changers) to gain job-ready skills with a modest time and cost investment . *(Official page: grow.google)*

Microsoft SC-900 (Security, Compliance, and Identity Fundamentals) – An entry-level Microsoft certification covering the basics of security, compliance, and identity (SCI) across Azure and Microsoft 365 services. SC-900 is great for understanding Azure AD, access management, security center, compliance manager, and related cloud security principles. It's often recommended for those pursuing Azure security or governance roles, as it "covers core principles in cloud, compliance, and identity" within Microsoft environments. *(Official Microsoft page: learn.microsoft.com)*

Offensive Security Certified Professional (OSCP) – A widely respected hands-on penetration testing certification from Offensive Security. To earn OSCP, candidates must complete a 24-hour practical exam where they successfully attack and penetrate various live machines in a controlled lab environment and produce a report. The OSCP is known as a rigorous test of real-world hacking skills (enumeration, exploitation, post-exploitation) and is often considered a milestone achievement for offensive security professionals. *(Official OffSec page: offsec.com)*

Splunk Core Certified User – An entry-level certification from Splunk that validates basic proficiency with Splunk's search and data analytics platform. It demonstrates an individual's ability to navigate the Splunk interface, run searches, use fields, create alerts/reports, and build dashboards. This "strong understanding of Splunk Enterprise and Splunk Cloud basics" is a common requirement for junior SIEM or security analyst roles working with Splunk. *(Official Splunk page: splunk.com)*

Tools and Technologies

Burp Suite (Community Edition) – A popular web application security testing tool. Burp Suite is used to find vulnerabilities in web apps by intercepting and modifying HTTP requests/responses. The free Community Edition provides core features like the intercepting proxy, repeater, and scanner (with some limitations), making it an essential tool for learning web app hacking and doing CTFs. *(Official site: portswigger.net)*

Kali Linux – A Debian-based Linux distribution preloaded with hundreds of penetration testing and cybersecurity tools. Kali includes tools for network scanning, exploitation, password cracking, forensics, and more (e.g. Nmap, Metasploit, John the Ripper). It is maintained by Offensive Security and is considered the standard OS for offensive security professionals due to its comprehensive toolset. *(Official site: kali.org)*

Nessus – A vulnerability assessment tool (developed by Tenable) that scans systems for security issues. Nessus can identify missing patches, misconfigurations, and common weaknesses on hosts, producing detailed reports. It's widely used by auditors and security teams for routine vulnerability scanning. *(Official site: tenable.com)*

Nmap – An open-source network scanner used to discover hosts and services on a computer network. Nmap (Network Mapper) can enumerate open ports, running services, OS versions, and more by sending crafted packets and analyzing responses. It's a fundamental tool for reconnaissance in both offensive and defensive contexts and is often one of the first tools a cybersecurity student learns to use. *(Official site:*

nmap.org)

Oracle VM VirtualBox – A free and open-source virtualization platform from Oracle. VirtualBox allows you to run multiple virtual machines (VMs) on a single physical host, which is extremely useful for building a home lab. For example, an aspiring analyst might run a Kali Linux VM and a vulnerable Windows VM on VirtualBox to practice attacks and defenses in a contained environment. *(Official site: virtualbox.org)*

Security Onion – A specialized Linux distribution for intrusion detection, enterprise security monitoring, and log management. Security Onion bundles many tools (Elastic stack, Zeek, Snort/Suricata, OSQuery, Wazuh, etc.) into one platform, allowing users to set up a home SOC environment. It's an all-in-one distro to practice blue team skills like analyzing network traffic, detecting threats, and investigating alerts. *(Official site: securityonion.net)*

Splunk (Free Version) – Splunk is a powerful Security Information and Event Management (SIEM) and log analysis platform. The free version of Splunk allows indexing and searching a limited amount of data per day, which is great for learning purposes. Aspiring SOC analysts use it to ingest logs and practice writing search queries, building dashboards, and detecting anomalies
. *(Official site: splunk.com)*

VMware Workstation Player – A free desktop virtualization software from VMware. Similar to VirtualBox, Workstation Player lets you run virtual machines on a PC (Windows or Linux host). It's often used to create isolated lab environments for practicing with different operating systems and security tools. For instance, one might run an intentionally vulnerable VM (like Metasploitable) in VMware and attack it from another VM. *(Official site: vmware.com)*

Wireshark – A free and open-source network protocol analyzer. Wireshark allows you to capture and interactively browse network traffic (packet capture). It's used to inspect network protocols at a very granular level, which is invaluable for troubleshooting, malware analysis, or incident response. For example, a defender might use Wireshark to analyze PCAP files and identify malicious traffic or exfiltrated data. *(Official site: wireshark.org)*

Organizations and Communities

(ISC)² (International Information System Security Certification Consortium) – A nonprofit membership association renowned for its cybersecurity certifications and education programs. (ISC)² is best known for certifications like CISSP, CCSP, and SSCP, which are globally respected. The organization also provides training, networking events, and research for the infosec community. *(Official site: isc2.org)*

CompTIA (Computing Technology Industry Association) – A leading nonprofit trade association that produces vendor-neutral IT certifications and advocates for the global tech workforce. CompTIA's certifications (such as A+, Network+, Security+, CySA+) are foundational in IT and cybersecurity career paths. CompTIA also offers training materials, publishes research, and hosts events to support IT professionals. *(Official site: comptia.org)*

EC-Council (International Council of E-Commerce Consultants) – A global cybersecurity education and certification organization, known as the creator of the Certified Ethical Hacker (CEH) certification. EC-Council offers a range of certs in ethical hacking, digital forensics, incident handling, and more. It is one of the world's largest technical cybersecurity certification bodies and also hosts conferences like Global CyberLympics. *(Official site: eccouncil.org)*

ISACA (Information Systems Audit and Control Association) – An international professional association focused on IT governance, audit, and security. ISACA offers globally recognized certifications including CISA, CISM, CRISC (Risk Management), and CGEIT (IT Governance). It provides members with training, research, and a community in areas of audit, risk, cybersecurity, and privacy "with knowledge, credentials, training and community" in these fields. *(Official site: isaca.org)*

Offensive Security (OffSec) – A private company known for its hands-on cybersecurity training and certifications, as well as for maintaining Kali Linux. Offensive Security's motto of "Try Harder" is reflected in their courses and cert exams (like OSCP, OSCE, etc.) which emphasize real-world pentesting skills. OffSec has become an industry standard for offensive training; its certifications are "some of the highest regarded in the industry."
(Official site: offsec.com)

OWASP (Open Web Application Security Project) – A worldwide nonprofit organization dedicated to improving the security of software, particularly web applications. OWASP is an open community that produces free resources: tools, documentation, forums, and famously the OWASP Top 10 (a regularly updated list of the most critical web security risks). They also have local chapters and host global AppSec conferences. *(Official site: owasp.org)*

SANS Institute – A highly respected organization providing cybersecurity training, certifications, and research. Founded in 1989, SANS offers intensive training courses taught by experts and runs events like the SANS summits. SANS is also the parent organization of GIAC certifications and develops the SANS Reading Room and Internet Storm Center. It is often regarded as "the largest source for information security training and security certification in the world."*(Official site: sans.org)*

(Additional community resources mentioned in the book include Reddit's r/cybersecurity and r/netsecstudents forums, various InfoSec Discord servers (e.g. InfoSec Prep, Blue Team Village), local ISSA/OWASP chapter meetups, and more – all great ways to network and learn informally in the cybersecurity community.)

Industry Reports and Statistics

Cybersecurity Ventures – A cybersecurity research firm known for its market reports and forecasts. Cybersecurity Ventures publishes widely cited statistics on cybercrime costs and job demand. For example, they reported that cybercrime will cost the world $10.5 trillion annually by 2025, and that there are over 3.5 million unfilled cybersecurity jobs worldwide. Their reports and articles are used to illustrate industry trends and the urgent need for cybersecurity talent. *(Website: cybersecurityventures.com)*

Palo Alto Networks Unit 42 Ransomware Report (2023) – An authoritative annual report on ransomware trends published by Unit 42, the threat intelligence team at Palo Alto Networks. The 2023 report revealed striking findings, such as the average ransom payment exceeding $1.5 million per incident. It covers ransomware group tactics, prevalent strains, ransom demands, and recommendations. This report is often referenced to understand the current state of ransomware and cyber extortion. *(Press release and full report: paloaltonetworks.com)*

U.S. Bureau of Labor Statistics (BLS) – The principal fact-finding agency for U.S. labor market data, cited for cybersecurity job outlook. The BLS projects information security analyst roles to grow over 30% from 2022 to 2032, much faster than the average for all occupations. This statistic is frequently mentioned to emphasize the strong demand and career opportunity in cybersecurity. *(BLS Occupational Outlook: bls.gov)*

Books and Guides

Blue Team Field Manual (BTFM) – *by Alan J. White & Ben Clark*. A compact reference guide for cyber defense practitioners (the "blue team"). It's packed with command-line tips, checklists, and best practices for tasks like log analysis, network monitoring, incident response, and forensic analysis. Often used as a quick-reference handbook during investigations or in a SOC environment. *(ISBN 9781541016363)*

Cybersecurity Career Master Plan – *by Dr. Gerald Auger, et al.* A guide aimed at helping readers break into the cybersecurity field and advance their careers. It covers creating a personal learning plan, networking, resume building, and obtaining the right skills and certifications for various cyber career paths. This book is written in an approachable style for those transitioning into cybersecurity, offering practical advice and resources. *(ISBN 9781801071706)*

Hacking: The Art of Exploitation – *by Jon Erickson.* A classic book (2nd Edition) that delves into the technical underpinnings of computer security and exploitation. It covers topics like C programming, buffer overflows, memory manipulation, shellcode, and cryptography, often with example code. This book is more advanced and low-level, teaching readers how exploits actually work under the hood. It's highly regarded for those interested in exploit development or understanding the art of hacking at a deeper level. *(ISBN 9781593271442)*

The Pentester Blueprint – *by Phillip L. Wylie & Kim Crawley.* A roadmap for anyone aspiring to become a penetration tester. It outlines the skills, certifications, and knowledge base required for pentesting, and offers guidance on how to gain experience (through labs, CTFs, bug bounties, etc.). The book also discusses different specialties within offensive security and how to build a personal brand/portfolio as an ethical hacker. *(ISBN 9781119684305)*

Influential Figures & Channels

IppSec (YouTube) – A well-known YouTube channel/persona in the hacking community. IppSec is renowned for its in-depth Hack The Box walkthrough videos. On his channel, he takes viewers through the process of enumerating and exploiting vulnerable HTB machines step-by-step. These videos are excellent for learning practical pentesting techniques and tools, as he explains his methodology for each challenge. *(YouTube: IppSec channel)*

John Hammond (YouTube) – A cybersecurity researcher and content creator who produces free educational videos on topics ranging from CTF challenges and malware analysis to tool tutorials and career advice. John Hammond's channel (with nearly 2 million subscribers) is popular for its hands-on walkthroughs and clear explanations; he often breaks down complex concepts in a beginner-friendly way, making cybersecurity more accessible. *(YouTube: John Hammond channel)*

NetworkChuck (YouTube) – A hugely popular IT/cybersecurity YouTuber with an energetic style. NetworkChuck covers everything from networking and cloud to hacking and coffee. His cybersecurity videos often focus on fun, practical projects — like setting up hacking labs, using Linux tools, or learning Python for security — presented in an engaging manner. With millions of followers, he's introduced many newcomers to cybersecurity and IT through his content. *(YouTube: NetworkChuck channel)*

These resources and references serve as a launchpad for further exploration. Whether you're learning through online platforms, pursuing certifications, honing skills with tools, participating in the community, or keeping up with industry reports and influencers, each resource listed here can play a role in your cybersecurity career journey. Stay curious and keep learning!

CONNECT WITH ME

www.cybtrps.com

www.ingramcontent.com/pod-product-compliance
Lightning Source LLC
LaVergne TN
LVHW022346060326
832902LV00022B/4276